LIFE IN THE UK TEST

THE COMPLETE STUDY GUIDE

OFFICIAL STUDY MATERIAL

+ REVISION GUIDE

+ 12 COMPLETE TESTS OFFICIAL STYLE

OVER 300 QUESTIONS

3RD EDITION - MAY 2019

DUX
PUBLISHING

First published September 2016
Third Edition May 2019

ISBN: 978-1-911538-18-9

Copyright © 2019 Dux Publishing. All rights reserved.
Dux Publishing is an imprint of Dux Enterprises Limited

All rights reserved. Apart from any permitted use under UK copyright law, no part of this publication may be reproduced or transmitted in any form or by any means, electronic or mechanical, including photocopying, recording, or any information, storage or retrieval system, without permission in writing from the publisher or under licence from the Copyright Licensing Agency Limited. Further details of such licenses (for reprographic reproduction) may be obtained from the Copyright Licensing Agency Ltd, Saffron House, 6-10 Kirby Street, London EC1N 8TS.

The author and publisher of this Book and the accompanying materials have used their best efforts in preparing this eBook. The author and publisher make no representation or warranties with respect to the accuracy, applicability, fitness, or completeness of the contents of this eBook. The information contained in this eBook is strictly for educational purposes. Therefore, if you wish to apply ideas contained in this eBook, you are taking full responsibility for your actions. The author and publisher disclaim any warranties (express or implied), merchantability, or fitness for any particular purpose. The author and publisher shall in no event be held liable to any party for any direct, indirect, punitive, special, incidental or other consequential damages arising directly or indirectly from any use of this material, which is provided "as is", and without warranties. As always, the advice of a competent legal, tax, accounting or other professional should be sought. The author and publisher do not warrant the performance, effectiveness or applicability of any sites listed or linked to in this eBook. All links are for information purposes only and are not warranted for content, accuracy or any other implied or explicit purpose.

Substantial material in this guide is crown copyright and has been obtained from the government publication Life in the United Kingdom: A Guide for New Residents (ISBN 978-0-11-341340-9). This information is reproduced with the permission of The National Archives under the Open Government License.

TABLE OF CONTENT

What is this guide about?	5
The values and principles of the UK	6
The Life in the UK test	7
How to use this book	10

OFFICIAL COURSE MATERIAL

A long and illustrious history	17
Early Britain	17
The Middle Ages	20
The Tudors and Stuarts	23
A global power	29
The 20th century	39
Britain since 1945	42
A modern, thriving society	53
The UK today	53
Religion	55
Customs and traditions	57
Sport	59
Arts and culture	63
Leisure	69
Places of interest	73
The UK government, the law and your role	81
The development of British democracy	81
The British constitution	82
The government	86
Who can vote?	90
The UK and international institutions	93
The European Union	93
Respecting the law	94
The role of the courts	97
Fundamental principles	100
Taxation	101
Driving	103
Your role in the community	103
How you can support your community	104
Looking after the environment	107

REVISION NOTES

Monarchs	112
English Kings	112
Norman Kings	113
Plantagenet Kings	113
Monarchs of England and Wales	113
House of Lancaster	113
House of York	114
The Tudors	114
The Stuarts	114
The Commonwealth	114
The Restoration	115
The Hanovarians	115
House of Windsor	115
Key Dates	116
Important people	121
UK population	123

TESTS

Official style tests	125
Test 1	127
Test 2	132
Test 3	137
Test 4	142
Test 5	147
Test 6	152
Test 7	157
Test 8	162
Test 9	167
Test 10	172
Test 11	177
Test 12	182
Answers to tests	187

WHAT IS THIS GUIDE ABOUT?

Are you looking to become a British citizen or to settle in the UK? Then if you are aged between 18 and 65 you will need to pass the Life in the UK test.

The test consists of many questions about the history of the UK, the country's traditions and customs as well as the rules of modern politics and institutions. You probably bought the book to study at your own pace, but if you are anything like me, you will prefer short notes, straight to the point and holding only the important facts without too much wording. This is exactly what I offer you in this guide: the facts, key dates and the information you need to go the test centre in confidence.

Third Edition 2019

Following the referendum in June 2016, the UK has decided to leave the European Union (EU). The sections relating to the EU in the book have been updated, but please note the following points *(this is not about politics, but about passing the test itself)*.

As of May 2019, the UK is still a member of the EU and nothing has changed yet.
When the UK leaves the EU (Potentially by 31st October 2019), certain legislations may be affected and parts of this book will then be updated.

Therefore, please do remember that any questions on Europe or the EU will consider the current position of the UK, not the future one. For instance, if you are asked whether the UK is part of the EU, for now, the correct answer is still YES.

THE VALUES AND PRINCIPLES OF THE UK

British society is founded on fundamental values and principles which all those living in the UK should respect and support. These values are reflected in the responsibilities, rights and privileges of being a British citizen or permanent resident of the UK. They are based on history and traditions and are protected by law, customs and expectations. There is no place in British society for extremism or intolerance.

The fundamental principles of British life include:
- Democracy
- The rule of law
- Individual liberty
- Tolerance of those with different faiths and beliefs
- Participation in community life.

As part of the citizenship ceremony, new citizens pledge to uphold these values. The pledge is:

> 'I will give my loyalty to the United Kingdom and respect its rights and freedoms. I will uphold its democratic values. I will observe its laws faithfully and fulfil my duties and obligations as a British citizen.'

The citizenship ceremony also request the new British citizen to take either an Oath of allegiance or an Affirmation of allegiance. By the Oath, you swear by Almighty God whereas with the Affirmation, you solemnly, sincerely and truly declare your allegiance to Her Majesty Queen Elizabeth the Second, her Heirs and Successors, according to law.

Flowing from the fundamental principles are responsibilities and freedoms which are shared by all those living in the UK and which we expect all residents to respect.

In return, the UK offers:

- freedom of belief and religion
- freedom of speech
- freedom from unfair discrimination
- a right to a fair trial
- a right to join in the election of a government.

THE LIFE IN THE UK TEST

No matter how much you already know about the UK, you will need to sit and pass the test as part of your application to live in the UK. To maximise your chances of passing, you may buy the book and study it either alone, online, in classes, or with a personal teacher. Then, when you are ready you can sit the exam and hopefully pass.

Remember, you do not need to pass the test if you are under 18 or over 64.

If you have already passed the test once, you do not need to sit again. For instance, if you have already passed the test to become settled in the UK and are now applying for citizenship, you do not need to sit the test again.

These are the three steps to ensure the best chances of success:

STUDY – BOOK – TAKE

First step: Study British customs, traditions and history

There is no secret here, a test is a test! The more you prepare for it, the greater your chances of success. In this guide, I provide some additional revision lists to help you prepare. You can carry it all with you in your kindle, on your phone, everywhere you want but be careful, you will not be allowed to take it to the test centre!
In the next few pages, I will give you some tips on the best way to prepare using this book and other resources.
But remember that ultimately, you know better than anyone else how you prefer to learn and memorise things.

Second step: Book the test

You must book the test at the very least three days in advance. I would suggest you book it several weeks in advance. This way, it gives you time to study but also a deadline. If you have a tendency to wait until last minute, you may never book the test at all. If you put a date in your calendar, then you know you need to be ready for that date. You can only book the test online! To book a test you need an email address, a debit or credit card, and a valid ID. If going online or using an email address is an issue, your local library, a university, or even a friend might help you with this part of the process.

Book the test here:
https://www.lituktestbooking.co.uk/lituk-web/

There are 60 official centres throughout the UK and you need to choose one close to where you live. You can choose among the five closest to you. Do not select another one as you may not be accepted on the day. The test will cost £50 independently of date and location. Be careful though, there is no refund so make sure you are making the correct booking and that you actually turn up on the day!

If you have any disabilities or special requirements, you should mention this at the time of booking the test. For any issue, there is a phone helpline available during the week.

Third step: Take the test

The test takes place in a room where no book or assistance materials are allowed. You will need to rely solely on your knowledge and memory. You cannot bring anyone with you. If you travelled with your children for instance, they will have to wait for you outside. Likewise, watches and electronic devices including phones are not accepted in the test room. There are lockers where you can securely leave these devices. Be careful, you will be searched on arrival, and cheating is a serious offence, which would not only void your test, but could also severely limit your application for settlement or citizenship.

When you arrive at the test centre, make sure you bring the following:

- The ID that you used to book the test online
- A proof of address less than 3 months old that shows your name and postcode

Cancellation

It is possible to cancel the test at least three days prior to the booked date. You can cancel online following the same process as you did to book it.

The test itself

There are 24 randomly selected questions about British traditions, history, and customs. You will have 45 minutes to reply to all of them. To be successful you will need to score 75% or more; meaning you must answer at least 18 of the 24 questions correctly. If you fail, you must wait seven days before you can sit and try again. There is no limitation to the amount of times you can sit the test, but you must pay the £50 fee every time.

---

24 random questions

45 minutes

75% score (= 18 correct answers)

Type of questions

There are four types of questions. See the example below.

1. One choice
   The question lists four possible options, only one is correct.

   On which day is Saint George celebrated?

   A. 22nd November
   B. 21st April
   C. 23rd April
   D. 1st March

   Answer: C

2. Multiple choice
   The question lists four options, and at least two can be correct.

   Which TWO of the following group are British Athletes?
   A. Winston Churchill
   B. Mo Farrah
   C. Richard Branson
   D. Dame Kelly Holmes

   Answer: B and D

3. True or false
   The question is a statement that is either true or false.

   Is the following statement true or false?

   The Prime Minister is appointed by the Parliament every 5 years.
   A. TRUE
   B. FALSE

   Answer: B

4. Find the correct statement
   The question lists two statements, but only one is correct.

   Which of the following statement is correct?

   A. The Wars of the Roses confirmed the independence of Scotland
   B. The Wars of the Roses established Henry Tudor on the throne of England

   Answer: B

HOW TO USE THIS BOOK

A few tips on learning the material, and passing the test.

The Life in the UK Test is no different from many other tests. As you enter the room and sit at the computer to answer the 24 questions, what you need can be summarised in two words: memory and confidence.

Memory is essential for success. The test is first and foremost a test of memory; it will ask you to find answers to questions based on the knowledge you have retained. For instance, if you are asked about the battle of Bosworth, you will need to remember it was fought in 1485. It saw the end of the Wars of Roses, the death of Richard III and the start of the Tudor dynasty by the accession to the throne of Henry VII. All this requires memory.

Confidence is also crucial in making you successful. The last thing you want during the test is to panic and forget names or get confused in the dates.

I will now give you a few tips for both.
Before I start, let me remind you of a single truth: hard work pays off. Don't listen to anyone who tells you otherwise. To pass an exam requires you to work at it. Learn, practice, spend some time revising what you know, and you will give yourself the best chances to pass.

Plan your learning

It is a simple trick that works well for many people: create a plan of action before you start learning. Get a deadline, cut the book in chunks of work, establish a routine, include intermediary milestones, test yourself at various points, check that you are on track, etc.

Regular bite size
Learn a little and often. Only a few people manage to learn a lot very fast. That is quite impressive, but not common. For most of us, what works is to progress little by little over some time. Don't put yourself in a position where you must learn the whole book in 2 days! Plan to do a couple of pages every day for a while.

Create a deadline
It may work better if you know there is an end date. For some people, it may be hard to commit to regular work until there is an end date. Then they realise they have to complete by that date. If that is you, what you can do is book the test. Book it weeks in advance, and then plan your learning. You always have the option to cancel if you need it.

Reward yourself
Don't forget to give yourself a little reward every now and then, especially when you achieve some milestone. For instance, if you pass a mock test, or when you finish one chapter of the book.

Memory

Divide & conquer
There are a lot of facts in this book. A lot of dates, names, numbers and other snippets of information to retain. Cut them into sections, parts. Don't attempt to learn all at once. For instance, in the history section, don't just learn every date in chronological order. That's way too much. Instead, just focus on a particular period. Like the Wars of the Roses or the Victorian era. Move onto the next section only when you know this one very well.

Pictures
We have all heard it before, a picture is worth a thousand words. Maybe you can draw your own. The book doesn't include that many pictures or photos, but it doesn't stop you from finding others for instance on the Internet. You can also draw your own diagrams to help memorise certain elements.

Practice with a friend or partner
Give the book to someone and let them ask you questions from the text. This can be a fun way to check what you know. Play it like a Trivial Pursuit if you wish.

Speak aloud
Speaking the text aloud can help you
We humans tend to remember what we hear more efficiently than what we read. It also works when we are talking to ourselves. Strange as it sounds, let's make use of this faculty.

Record yourself
To encourage your learning by listening, you can record yourself and then, for instance, listen back during your commute. There are many free apps on smartphones that can help you there.

Right before you go to bed
We tend to retain easily the information we absorb just before we go to sleep. It is quite common to read or listen to something important in bed, then sleep on it.

Start with the end or repeat randomly
An alternative method of learning a long text is to repeat it in reverse! Once you know a section of the book, revise or check your knowledge not in order, but from the end of the chapter, or even randomly.

Understand the meaning
There is no secret here, it is helpful to understand well what you are trying to commit to memory! For instance, the judicial system in the UK can be a bit difficult to grasp, especially if you come from a country that has a different approach. Use a dictionary and websites to read about it more and make sure you really understand how the various courts work.

Listen as you drive, commute, walk in the park...
Driving or taking the train to work can take a fair chunk of our free time. why not use that time in a useful manner? Lsiten to the audiobook (or your own recording) as you commute.

It can sometimes help to walk while listening to the course. A bit like mindfulness, where you focus on the present, on your surroundings, on your sensations. Walking is an activity that often allows us to clear our mind. Then, put on your earplugs and listen to the course. It may help sink it in.

Write it down
It is a simple tip, but sometimes writing the text down helps to commit it to memory. Now, a word of caution: don't attempt to rewrite the whole book, that would take some time! Instead, write down a few notes, essential words, dates, characters etc.

A useful tool to learn is a flashcard. For instance, write a word on one side and its definition or what it relates to on the other side. Then read one side and ask yourself the other.

Confidence

Confidence is vital to increase your chance of passing an exam. But it is also quite hard to get if you have test-phobia.

The first thing to note is that if you know the content well, you increase your confidence. It is quite simple: go to a test centre with limited knowledge, and you are likely to panic. Work at it and know it well and you are more likely to feel good.

The test itself will see you sat alone at a computer under supervision. If you are not used to it, familiarise yourself by taking online tests (there are loads!) and getting used to reading on a screen and using the mouse.

Read the question calmly. Make sure you understand what is asked. Especially if it is a true or false statement, make sure it is not, for instance, a double negative (such as: "it is not uncommon" means it is common). Now read the possible answers. Read the question again. If one answer jumps at you, great. If not, try to eliminate any answer you know is incorrect.

If you are still uncertain, trust your instinct. Sometimes we ignore our hunches, but they are often correct.

You can jump to another question and mark this one for later. At the end of the test, you have the possibility to review all the questions and your answers. Now, my advice is to be cautious here... very often, when we doubt a response, we end up changing it wrongly.

Time management
You have 45 minutes for 24 questions. I would suggest you work on 40 minutes. That gives you 5 minutes buffer if you need to review a question or think about one of your answers. It means you have about 1.5 minutes per question. It feels little time, but if you pace yourself, it is actually a lot of time. It will take you about 3 to 10 seconds to read the question and up to 20 seconds to read the answers. You now have over a minute to pick the answer. It is enough time. Think about it, it will have taken you between 15 and 30 seconds to read this paragraph. If you spend too long on a question, you will panic over the answer. After 1 minute, just move on and come back later.

You
The test is yours. Only you will be facing the computer. Nobody is judging you. Breath, try to relax. Remember, it is just a test, not like you are undergoing heart surgery.
You can sit several times. You will pass it.

On the day
Here are a few tips for the day of the test:
- Get to the centre early. They will not admit you last minute, and you should spend a couple of minutes sitting in there, breathing and calming your whole body down.
- Don't take anything you don't need. You will have to leave your wallet, phone etc. in a locker, so go to the centre as light as you can.
- On a hot day, sit for a bit, cool down before entering the room.
- Drink a bit of water before the test.
- Go to the toilets.
- Maybe book in the morning if you can so you don't spend the whole day thinking about it.
- Take tissue with you, you don't want to panic over not being able to blow your nose when you need to.
- Organise something to look forward to, right after the test. Drinks, meet a friend, shopping... like a reward.
- Say hello to the people you meet, say a nice word. First, it never hurts to be polite but also, it gets you in a positive frame of mind.
- Don't revise on the day. Some people like doing it, but if you know your stuff, you know it. Clear your mind for the day.
- Have a nice breakfast or lunch. Give yourself something you like before the test, it will make you feel good.
- If you have to travel to the centre, see if someone can accompany you. Talk with them, but not about the test!

Final words

This book that you have in your hands, on your electronic device or that you are listening to contains 100% of the official course material published by the Home Office and a series of mock exams to help you prepare.

All the books on the Life in the UK test contain the exact same course. The material has been written by the Home Office, and publishers are not authorised to change it. There is no need to buy another Life In the UK book to supplement your learning because you would re-read the same. Instead, browse the web to find useful information. For instance, when locations are quoted, go online to check what they look like. This book will help you, but you are free to get more information from other places too.

There are many websites to help you practice questions. The official writers of the test have to ensure that it is possible to answer their questions with the Life in The UK content only, but it is possible that one rogue question goes through the checks and requires more knowledge. This is rare but is known to have happened. Don't panic, there would only be one like this, and you might know the answer anyway.

This book is available on **Paperback**, **eBook** and **AudioBook**.

The Official Material for the

LIFE IN THE UK TEST

Course developed by the Home Office
and published by the TSO (The Stationery Office).

A LONG AND ILLUSTRIOUS HISTORY

In this chapter you will learn about British history starting from the Stone Age. The beginning focuses on arriving populations which affected the language and religions of Britain. After that the focus is on the development of the Monarchy, church and Parliament. Major battles and significant periods are covered, including the civil war, the industrial revolution and the Empire. There is a lot of information about WWI and WWII and after WWII the chapter focuses on the governments of the UK and devolution in Northern Ireland, Wales and Scotland.

Make sure that you know and understand:
- the early populations of Britain,
- the relationship between the Monarchy and Parliament,
- Protestants and Catholics,
- Britain and the colonies of the Empire,
- how the right to vote developed,
- the Acts of Parliament and other major events,
- all of the dates given in this chapter.

Early Britain

The first people to live in Britain were hunter-gatherers, in what we call the Stone Age. For much of the Stone Age, Britain was connected to the continent by a land bridge. People came and went, following the herds of deer and horses which they hunted. Britain only became permanently separated from the continent by the Channel about 10,000 years ago.

The first farmers arrived in Britain about 6,000 years ago. The ancestors of these first farmers probably came from south-east Europe. These people built houses, tombs and monuments on the land. One of these monuments, Stonehenge, still stands in what is now the English county of Wiltshire. Stonehenge was probably a special gathering place for seasonal ceremonies. Other Stone Age sites have also survived. Skara Brae on Orkney, off the north coast of Scotland, is the best preserved prehistoric village in northern Europe, and has helped archaeologists to understand more about how people lived near the end of the Stone Age.

Around 4,000 years ago, people learned to make bronze. We call this period the Bronze Age. People lived in roundhouses and buried their dead in tombs called round barrows. The people of the Bronze Age were accomplished metalworkers who made many beautiful objects in bronze and gold, including tools, ornaments and weapons. The Bronze Age was followed by the Iron Age, when people learned how to make weapons and tools out of iron. People still lived in roundhouses, grouped together into larger settlements, and sometimes defended sites called hill forts. A very impressive hill fort can still be seen today at Maiden Castle, in the English county of Dorset. Most people were farmers, craft workers or warriors. The language they spoke was part of the Celtic language family. Similar languages were spoken across Europe in the Iron Age, and related languages are still spoken today in some parts of Wales, Scotland and Ireland. The people of the Iron Age had a sophisticated culture and economy. They made the first coins to be minted in Britain, some inscribed with the names of Iron Age kings. This marks the beginnings of British history.

The Romans
Julius Caesar led a Roman invasion of Britain in 55 BC. This was unsuccessful and for nearly 100 years Britain remained separate from the Roman Empire. In AD 43 the Emperor Claudius led the Roman army in a new invasion. This time, there was resistance from some of the British tribes but the Romans were successful in occupying almost all of Britain. One of the tribal leaders who fought against the Romans was Boudicca, the queen of the Iceni in what is now eastern England. She is still remembered today and there is a statue of her on Westminster Bridge in London, near the Houses of Parliament.

Areas of what is now Scotland were never conquered by the Romans, and the Emperor Hadrian built a wall (*see photo*) in the north of England to keep out the Picts (ancestors of the Scottish people). Included in the wall were a number of forts. Parts of Hadrian's Wall, including the forts of Housesteads and Vindolanda, can still be seen. It is a popular area for walkers and is a UNESCO (United Nations Education, Scientific and Cultural Organization) World Heritage Site.

The Romans remained in Britain for 400 years. They built roads and public buildings, created a structure of law, and introduced new plants and animals. It was during the 3rd and 4th centuries AD that the first Christian communities began to appear in Britain.

The Anglo-Saxons
The Roman army left Britain in AD 410 to defend other parts of the Roman Empire and never returned. Britain was again invaded by tribes from northern Europe: the Jutes, the Angles and the Saxons. The languages they spoke are the basis of modern-day English. Battles were fought against these invaders but, by about AD 600, Anglo-Saxon kingdoms were established in Britain. These kingdoms were mainly in what is now England. The

burial place of one of the kings was at Sutton Hoo in modern Suffolk. This king was buried with treasure and armour, all placed in a ship which was then covered by a mound of earth. Parts of the west of Britain, including much of what is now Wales, and Scotland, remained free of Anglo-Saxon rule.

The Anglo-Saxons were not Christians when they first came to Britain but, during this period, missionaries came to Britain to preach about Christianity. Missionaries from Ireland spread the religion in the north. The most famous of these were St Patrick, who would become the patron saint of Ireland (see patron saints), and St Columba, who founded a monastery on the island of Iona, off the coast of what is now Scotland. St Augustine led missionaries from Rome, who spread Christianity in the south. St Augustine became the first Archbishop of Canterbury (see the Archbishop of Canterbury and the Church in Britain today).

The Vikings

The Vikings came from Denmark and Norway. They first visited Britain in AD 789 to raid coastal towns and take away goods and slaves. Then, they began to stay and form their own communities in the east of England and Scotland. The Anglo-Saxon kingdoms in England united under King Alfred the Great, who defeated the Vikings. Many of the Viking invaders stayed in Britain – especially in the east and north of England, in an area known as the Danelaw (many places names there, such as Grimsby and Scunthorpe, come from the Viking languages). The Viking settlers mixed with local communities and some converted to Christianity.

Anglo-Saxon kings continued to rule what is now England, except for a short period when there were Danish kings. The first of these was Cnut, also called Canute.

In the north, the threat of attack by Vikings had encouraged the people to unite under one king, Kenneth MacAlpin. The term Scotland began to be used to describe that country.

The Norman Conquest

In 1066, an invasion led by William, the Duke of Normandy (in what is now northern France), defeated Harold, the Saxon king of England, at the Battle of Hastings. Harold was killed in the battle. William became king of England and is known as William the Conqueror. The battle is commemorated in a great piece of embroidery, known as the Bayeux Tapestry, which can still be seen in France today.

The Norman Conquest was the last successful foreign invasion of England and led to many changes in government and social structures in England. Norman French, the language of the new ruling class, influenced the development of the English language as we know it today. Initially the Normans also conquered Wales, but the Welsh gradually won territory back. The Scots and the Normans fought on the border between England and Scotland; the Normans took over some land on the border but did not invade Scotland.

William sent people all over England to draw up lists of all the towns and villages. The people who lived there, who owned the land and what animals they owned were also listed. This was called the Domesday Book. It still exists today and gives a picture of society in England just after the Norman Conquest.

The Middle Ages

War at home and abroad
The period after the Norman Conquest up until about 1485 is called the Middle Ages (or the medieval period). It was a time of almost constant war.

The English kings fought with the Welsh, Scottish and Irish noblemen for control of their lands. In Wales, the English were able to establish their rule. In 1284 King Edward I of England introduced the Statute of Rhuddlan, which annexed Wales to the Crown of England. Huge castles, including Conwy and Caernarvon, were built to maintain this power. By the middle of the 15th century the last Welsh rebellions had been defeated. English laws and the English language were introduced.

In Scotland, the English kings were less successful. In 1314 the Scottish, led by Robert the Bruce, defeated the English at the Battle of Bannockburn, and Scotland remained unconquered by the English.

At the beginning of the Middle Ages, Ireland was an independent country. The English first went to Ireland as troops to help the Irish king and remained to build their own settlements. By 1200, the English ruled an area of Ireland known as the Pale, around Dublin. Some of the important lords in other parts of Ireland accepted the authority of the English king.

During the Middle Ages, the English kings also fought a number of wars abroad. Many knights took part in the Crusades, in which European Christians fought for control of the Holy Land. English kings also fought a long war with France, called the Hundred Years War (even though it actually lasted 116 years). One of the most famous battles of the Hundred Years War was the Battle of Agincourt in 1415, where King Henry V's vastly outnumbered English army defeated the French. The English left France in the 1450s.

The Black Death

The Normans used a system of land ownership known as feudalism. The king gave land to his lords in return for help in war. Landowners had to send certain numbers of men to serve in the army. Some peasants had their own land but most were serfs.

They had a small area of their lord's land where they could grow food. In return, they had to work for their lord and could not move away. The same system developed in southern Scotland. In the north of Scotland and Ireland, land was owned by members of the 'clans' (prominent families).

In 1348, a disease, probably a form of plague, came to Britain. This was known as the Black Death. One third of the population of England died and a similar proportion in Scotland and Wales. This was one of the worst disasters ever to strike Britain. Following the Black Death, the smaller population meant there was less need to grow cereal crops. There were labour shortages and peasants began to demand higher wages. New social classes appeared, including owners of large areas of land (later called the gentry), and people left the countryside to live in the towns. In the towns, growing wealth led to the development of a strong middle class.

In Ireland, the Black Death killed many in the Pale and, for a time, the area controlled by the English became smaller.

Legal and political changes

In the Middle Ages, Parliament began to develop into the institution it is today. Its origins can be traced to the king's council of advisers, which included important noblemen and the leaders of the Church.

There were few formal limits to the king's power until 1215. In that year, King John was forced by his noblemen to agree to a number of demands. The result was a charter of rights called the Magna Carta (which means the Great Charter). The Magna Carta established the idea that even the king was subject to the law. It protected the rights of the nobility and restricted the king's power to collect taxes or to make or change laws. In future, the king would need to involve his noblemen in decisions.

In England, parliaments were called for the king to consult his nobles, particularly when the king needed to raise money. The numbers attending Parliament increased and two separate parts, known as Houses, were established. The nobility, great landowners and bishops sat in the House of Lords. Knights, who were usually smaller landowners, and wealthy people from towns and cities were elected to sit in the House of Commons. Only a small part of the population was able to join in electing the members of the Commons.

A similar Parliament developed in Scotland. It had three Houses, called Estates: the lords, the commons and the clergy.

This was also a time of development in the legal system. The principle that judges are independent of the government began to be established. In England, judges developed 'common law' by a process of precedence (that is, following previous decisions) and tradition. In Scotland, the legal system developed slightly differently and laws were 'codified' (that is, written down).

A distinct identity

The Middle Ages saw the development of a national culture and identity. After the Norman Conquest, the king and his noblemen had spoken Norman French and the peasants had continued to speak Anglo-Saxon. Gradually these two languages combined to become one English language. Some words in modern English – for example, 'park' and 'beauty' – are based on Norman French words. Others – for example, 'apple', 'cow' and 'summer' – are based on Anglo-Saxon words. In modern English there are often words with very similar meanings, one from French and one from Anglo-Saxon. 'Demand' (French) and 'ask' (Anglo-Saxon) are examples. By 1400, in England, official documents were being written in English, and English had become the preferred language of the royal court and Parliament.

In the years leading up to 1400, Geoffrey Chaucer wrote a series of poems in English about a group of people going to Canterbury on a pilgrimage. The people decided to tell each other stories on the journey, and the poems describe the travellers and some of the stories they told. This collection of poems is called The Canterbury Tales. It was one of the first books to be printed by William Caxton, the first person in England to print books using a printing press. Many of the stories are still popular. Some have been made into plays and television programmes.

1400 - Geoffrey Chaucer wrote The Canterbury Tales - a series of poems.

In Scotland, many people continued to speak Gaelic and the Scots language also developed. A number of poets began to write in the Scots language. One example is John Barbour, who wrote The Bruce about the Battle of Bannockburn.

The Middle Ages also saw a change in the type of buildings in Britain. Castles were built in many places in Britain and Ireland, partly for defence. Today many are in ruins, although some, such as Windsor and Edinburgh, are still in use. Great cathedrals – for example, Lincoln Cathedral – were also built, and many of these are still used for worship. Several of the cathedrals had windows of stained glass, telling stories about the Bible and Christian saints. The glass in York Minster is a famous example.

During this period, England was an important trading nation. English wool became a very important export. People came to England from abroad to trade and also to work. Many had special skills, such as weavers from France, engineers from Germany, glass manufacturers from Italy and canal builders from Holland.

The Wars of the Roses

In 1455, a civil war was begun to decide who should be king of England. It was fought between the supporters of two families: the House of Lancaster and the House of York. This war was called the Wars of the Roses, because the symbol of Lancaster was a red rose and the symbol of York was a white rose. The war ended with the Battle of Bosworth Field in 1485.

King Richard III of the House of York was killed in the battle and Henry Tudor, the leader of the House of Lancaster, became King Henry VII. Henry then married King Richard's niece, Elizabeth of York, and united the two families. Henry was the first king of the House of Tudor. The symbol of the House of Tudor was a red rose with a white rose inside it as a sign that the Houses of York and Lancaster were now allies.

The Tudors and Stuarts

Religious conflicts

After his victory in the Wars of the Roses, Henry VII wanted to make sure that England remained peaceful and that his position as king was secure. He deliberately strengthened the central administration of England and reduced the power of the nobles. He was thrifty and built up the monarchy's financial reserves. When he died, his son Henry VIII continued the policy of centralising power.

Henry VIII was most famous for breaking away from the Church of Rome and marrying six times.

To divorce his first wife, Henry needed the approval of the Pope. When the Pope refused, Henry established the Church of England. In this new Church, the king, not the Pope, would have the power to appoint bishops and order how people should worship.

At the same time the Reformation was happening across Europe. This was a movement against the authority of the Pope and the ideas and practices of the Roman Catholic Church. The Protestants formed their own churches. They read the Bible in their own languages instead of in Latin; they did not pray to saints or at shrines; and they believed that a person's own relationship with God was more important than submitting to the authority of the Church. Protestant ideas gradually gained strength in England, Wales and Scotland during the 16th century.

In Ireland, however, attempts by the English to impose Protestantism (alongside efforts to introduce the English system of laws about the inheritance of land) led to rebellion from the Irish chieftains, and much brutal fighting followed.

During the reign of Henry VIII, Wales became formally united with England by the Act for the Government of Wales. The Welsh sent representatives to the House of Commons and the Welsh legal system was reformed.

Henry VIII was succeeded by his son Edward VI, who was strongly Protestant. During his reign, the Book of Common Prayer was written to be used in the Church of England. A version of this book is still used in some churches today. Edward died at the age of 15 after ruling for just over six years, and his half-sister Mary became queen. Mary was a devout Catholic and persecuted Protestants (for this reason, she became known as 'Bloody Mary'). Mary also died after a short reign and the next monarch was her half-sister, Elizabeth, the daughter of Henry VIII and Anne Boleyn.

Queen Elizabeth I

Queen Elizabeth I was a Protestant. She re-established the Church of England as the official Church in England. Everyone had to attend their local church and there were laws about the type of religious services and the prayers which could be said, but Elizabeth did not ask about people's real beliefs. She succeeded in finding a balance between the views of Catholics and the more extreme Protestants. In this way, she avoided any serious religious conflict within England. Elizabeth became one of the most popular monarchs in English history, particularly after 1588, when the English defeated the Spanish Armada (a large fleet of ships), which had been sent by Spain to conquer England and restore Catholicism.

The Reformation in Scotland and Mary, Queen of Scots

Scotland had also been strongly influenced by Protestant ideas. In 1560, the predominantly Protestant Scottish Parliament abolished the authority of the Pope in Scotland and Roman Catholic religious services became illegal. A Protestant Church of Scotland with a leadership was established but, unlike in England, this was not a state Church.

The queen of Scotland, Mary Stuart (often now called 'Mary, Queen of Scots') was a Catholic. She was only a week old when her father died and she became queen. Much of her childhood was spent in France. When she returned to Scotland, she was the centre of a power struggle between different groups. When her husband was murdered, Mary was suspected of involvement and fled to England. She gave her throne to her Protestant son, James VI of Scotland. Mary was Elizabeth I's cousin and hoped that Elizabeth might help her, but Elizabeth suspected Mary of wanting to take over the English throne, and kept her a prisoner for 20 years. Mary was eventually executed, accused of plotting against Elizabeth I.

Exploration, poetry and drama

The Elizabethan period in England was a time of growing patriotism: a feeling of pride in being English. English explorers sought new trade routes and tried to expand British trade into the Spanish colonies in the Americas. Sir Francis Drake, one of the commanders in the defeat of the Spanish Armada, was one of the founders of England's naval tradition. His ship, the Golden Hind, was one of the first to sail right around ('circumnavigate') the world. In Elizabeth I's time, English settlers first began to colonise the eastern coast of America. This colonisation, particularly by people who disagreed with the religious views

> **William Shakespeare (1564–1616)**
> Shakespeare was born in Stratford-upon-Avon, England. He was a playwright and actor and wrote many poems and plays. His most famous plays include *A Midsummer Night's Dream, Hamlet, Macbeth* and *Romeo and Juliet*. He also dramatised significant events from the past, but he did not focus solely on kings and queens. He was one of the first to portray ordinary Englishmen and women. Shakespeare had a great influence on the English language and invented many words that are still common today.
>
> Lines from his plays and poems which are often still quoted include:
> - Once more unto the breach (*Henry V*)
> - To be or not to be (*Hamlet*)
> - A rose by any other name (*Romeo and Juliet*)
> - All the world's a stage (*As You Like It*)
> - The darling buds of May (*Sonnet 18 – Shall I Compare Thee To a Summer's Day*).
>
> Many people regard Shakespeare as the greatest playwright of all time. His plays and poems are still performed and studied in Britain and other countries today. The Globe Theatre in London is a modern copy of the theatres in which his plays were first performed.

of the next two kings, greatly increased in the next century.

The Elizabethan period is also remembered for the richness of its poetry and drama, especially the plays and poems of William Shakespeare.

James VI and I

Elizabeth I never married and so had no children of her own to inherit her throne. When she died in 1603 her heir was her cousin James VI of Scotland. He became King James I of England, Wales and Ireland but Scotland remained a separate country.

The King James Bible

One achievement of King James' reign was a new translation of the Bible into English. This translation is known as the 'King James Version' or the 'Authorised Version'. It was not the first English Bible but is a version which continues to be used in many Protestant churches today.

Ireland

During this period, Ireland was an almost completely Catholic country. Henry VII and

Henry VIII had extended English control outside the Pale (see War at Home and Abroad) and had established English authority over the whole country. Henry VIII took the title 'King of Ireland'. English laws were introduced and local leaders were expected to follow the instructions of the Lord Lieutenants in Dublin.

During the reigns of Elizabeth I and James I, many people in Ireland opposed rule by the Protestant government in England. There were a number of rebellions. The English government encouraged Scottish and English Protestants to settle in Ulster, the northern province of Ireland, taking over the land from Catholic landholders. These settlements were known as plantations. Many of the new settlers came from south-west Scotland and other land was given to companies based in London. James later organised similar plantations in several other parts of Ireland. This had serious longterm consequences for the history of England, Scotland and Ireland.

The rise of Parliament
Elizabeth I was very skilled at managing Parliament. During her reign, she was successful in balancing her wishes and views against those of the House of Lords and those of the House of Commons, which was increasingly Protestant in its views.

James I and his son Charles I were less skilled politically. Both believed in the 'Divine Right of Kings': the idea that the king was directly appointed by God to rule. They thought that the king should be able to act without having to seek approval from Parliament. When Charles I inherited the thrones of England, Wales, Ireland and Scotland, he tried to rule in line with this principle. When he could not get Parliament to agree with his religious and foreign policies, he tried to rule without Parliament at all. For 11 years, he found ways in which to raise money without Parliament's approval but eventually trouble in Scotland meant that he had to recall Parliament.

The beginning of the English civil war
Charles I wanted the worship of the Church of England to include more ceremony and introduced a revised Prayer Book. He tried to impose this Prayer Book on the Presbyterian Church in Scotland and this led to serious unrest. A Scottish army was formed and Charles could not find the money he needed for his own army without the help of Parliament. In 1640, he recalled Parliament to ask it for funds. Many in Parliament were Puritans, a group of Protestants who advocated strict and simple religious doctrine and worship. They did not agree with the king's religious views and disliked his reforms of the Church of England. Parliament refused to give the king the money he asked for, even after the Scottish army invaded England.

Another rebellion began in Ireland because the Roman Catholics in Ireland were afraid of the growing power of the Puritans. Parliament took this opportunity to demand control of the English army – a change that would have transferred substantial power from the king to Parliament. In response, Charles I entered the House of Commons and tried to arrest five parliamentary leaders, but they had been warned and were not there. (No monarch has set foot in the Commons since.) Civil war between the king and Parliament could not now be avoided and began in 1642. The country split into those who supported the king (the Cavaliers) and those who supported Parliament (the Roundheads).

Oliver Cromwell and the English Republic

The king's army was defeated at the Battles of Marston Moor and Naseby. By 1646, it was clear that Parliament had won the war. Charles was held prisoner by the parliamentary army. He was still unwilling to reach any agreement with Parliament and in 1649 he was executed.

England declared itself a republic, called the Commonwealth. It no longer had a monarch. For a time, it was not totally clear how the country would be governed. For now, the army was in control. One of its generals, Oliver Cromwell, was sent to Ireland, where the revolt which had begun in 1641 still continued and where there was still a Royalist army. Cromwell was successful in establishing the authority of the English Parliament but did this with such violence that even today Cromwell remains a controversial figure in Ireland.

The Commonwealth, lead by Oliver Cromwell was a republic that started after the execution of King Charles I by Parlament in 1649.

The Scots had not agreed to the execution of Charles I and declared his son Charles II to be king. He was crowned king of Scotland and led a Scottish army into England. Cromwell defeated this army in the Battles of Dunbar and Worcester. Charles II escaped from Worcester, famously hiding in an oak tree on one occasion, and eventually fled to Europe. Parliament now controlled Scotland as well as England and Wales.

After his campaign in Ireland and victory over Charles II at Worcester, Cromwell was recognised as the leader of the new republic. He was given the title of Lord Protector and ruled until his death in 1658. When Cromwell died, his son, Richard, became Lord Protector in his place but was not able to control the army or the government. Although Britain had been a republic for 11 years, without Oliver Cromwell there was no clear leader or system of government. Many people in the country wanted stability. People began to talk about the need for a king.

The Restoration

In May 1660, Parliament invited Charles II to come back from exile in the Netherlands. He was crowned King Charles II of England, Wales, Scotland and Ireland. Charles II made it clear that he had 'no wish to go on his travels again'. He understood that he could not always do as he wished but would sometimes need to reach agreement with Parliament. Generally, Parliament supported his policies. The Church of England again became the established official Church. Both Roman Catholics and Puritans were kept out of power.

During Charles II's reign, in 1665, there was a major outbreak of plague in London. Thousands of people died, especially in poorer areas. The following year, a great fire destroyed much of the city, including many churches and St Paul's Cathedral. London was rebuilt with a new St Paul's, which was designed by a famous architect, Sir Christopher Wren. Samuel Pepys wrote about these events in a diary which was later published and is still read today.

The Habeas Corpus Act became law in 1679.

This was a very important piece of legislation which remains relevant today. Habeas corpus is Latin for 'you must present the person in court'. The Act guaranteed that no one could be held prisoner unlawfully. Every prisoner has a right to a court hearing.

Charles II was interested in science. During his reign, the Royal Society was formed to promote 'natural knowledge'. This is the oldest surviving scientific society in the world. Among its early members were Sir Edmund Halley, who successfully predicted the return of the comet now called Halley's Comet, and Sir Isaac Newton.

Isaac Newton (1643–1727)
Born in Lincolnshire, eastern England, Isaac Newton first became interested in science when he studied at Cambridge University. He became an important figure in the field. His most famous published work was Philosophiae Naturalis Principia Mathematica (*'Mathematical Principles of Natural Philosophy'*), which showed how gravity applied to the whole universe. Newton also discovered that white light is made up of the colours of the rainbow. Many of his discoveries are still important for modern science.

A Catholic King
Charles II had no legitimate children. He died in 1685 and his brother, James, who was a Roman Catholic, became King James II in England, Wales and Ireland and King James VII of Scotland. James favoured Roman Catholics and allowed them to be army Officers, which an Act of Parliament had forbidden. He did not seek to reach agreements with Parliament and arrested some of the bishops of the Church of England. People in England worried that James wanted to make England a Catholic country once more. However, his heirs were his two daughters, who were both firmly Protestant, and people thought that this meant there would soon be a Protestant monarch again. Then, James's wife had a son. Suddenly, it seemed likely that the next monarch would not be a Protestant after all.

The Glorious Revolution
James II's elder daughter, Mary, was married to her cousin William of Orange, the Protestant ruler of the Netherlands. In 1688, important Protestants in England asked

William to invade England and proclaim himself king. When William reached England, there was no resistance. James fled to France and William took over the throne, becoming William III in England, Wales and Ireland, and William II of Scotland. William ruled jointly with Mary. This event was later called the 'Glorious Revolution' because there was no fighting in England and because it guaranteed the power of Parliament, ending the threat of a monarch ruling on his or her own as he or she wished.

James II wanted to regain the throne and invaded Ireland with the help of a French army. William defeated James II at the Battle of the Boyne in Ireland in 1690, an event which is still celebrated by some in Northern Ireland today. William re-conquered Ireland and James fled back to France. Many restrictions were placed on the Roman Catholic Church in Ireland and Irish Catholics were unable to take part in the government.

There was also support for James in Scotland. An attempt at an armed rebellion in support of James was quickly defeated at Killiecrankie. All Scottish clans were required formally to accept William as king by taking an oath. The MacDonalds of Glencoe were late in taking the oath and were all killed. The memory of this massacre meant some Scots distrusted the new government.

Some continued to believe that James was the rightful king, particularly in Scotland. Some joined him in exile in France; others were secret supporters. James' supporters became known as Jacobites.

A global power

Constitutional monarchy – The Bill of Rights
At the coronation of William and Mary, a Declaration of Rights was read. This confirmed that the king would no longer be able to raise taxes or administer justice without agreement from Parliament. The balance of power between monarch and Parliament had now permanently changed. The Bill of Rights, 1689, confirmed the rights of Parliament and the limits of the king's power. Parliament took control of who could be monarch and declared that the king or queen must be a Protestant. A new Parliament had to be elected at least every three years (later this became seven years and now it is five years). Every year the monarch had to ask Parliament to renew funding for the army and the navy.

These changes meant that, to be able to govern effectively, the monarch needed to have advisers, or ministers, who would be able to ensure a majority of votes in the House of Commons and the House of Lords. There were two main groups in Parliament, known as the Whigs and the Tories. (The modern Conservative Party is still sometimes referred to as the Tories.) This was the beginning of party politics.

This was also an important time for the development of a free press (newspapers and other publications which are not controlled by the government). From 1695, newspapers were allowed to operate without a government licence. Increasing numbers of newspapers began to be published.

The laws passed after the Glorious Revolution are the beginning of what is called 'constitutional monarchy'. The monarch remained very important but was no longer able to insist on particular policies or actions if Parliament did not agree. After William III, the ministers gradually became more important than the monarch but this was not a democracy in the modern sense. The number of people who had the right to vote for members of Parliament was still very small. Only men who owned property of a certain value were able to vote. No women at all had the vote. Some constituencies were controlled by a single wealthy family. These were called 'pocket boroughs'. Other constituencies had hardly any voters and were called 'rotten boroughs'.

A growing population

This was a time when many people left Britain and Ireland to settle in new colonies in America and elsewhere, but others came to live in Britain. The first Jews to come to Britain since the Middle Ages settled in London in 1656. Between 1680 and 1720 many refugees called Huguenots came from France. They were Protestants and had been persecuted for their religion. Many were educated and skilled and worked as scientists, in banking, or in weaving or other crafts.

The Act of Treaty or Union in Scotland

William and Mary's successor, Queen Anne, had no surviving children. This created uncertainty over the succession in England, Wales and Ireland and in Scotland. The Act of Union, known as the Treaty of Union in Scotland, was therefore agreed in 1707, creating the Kingdom of Great Britain. Although Scotland was no longer an independent country, it kept its own legal and education systems and Presbyterian Church.

The Prime Minister

When Queen Anne died in 1714, Parliament chose a German, George I, to be the next king, because he was Anne's nearest Protestant relative. An attempt by Scottish Jacobites to put James II's son on the throne instead was quickly defeated. George I did not speak very good English and this increased his need to rely on his ministers. The most important minister in Parliament became known as the Prime Minister. The first man to be called this was Sir Robert Walpole, who was Prime Minister from 1721 to 1742.

Sir Robert Walpole was the first Prime Minister (1721 to 1742) under King George I.

The rebellion of the clans

In 1745 there was another attempt to put a Stuart king back on the throne in place of

George I's son, George II. Charles Edward Stuart (Bonnie Prince Charlie), the grandson of James II, landed in Scotland. He was supported by clansmen from the Scottish highlands and raised an army. Charles initially had some successes but was defeated by George II's army at the Battle of Culloden in 1746. Charles escaped back to Europe.

The clans lost a lot of their power and influence after Culloden. Chieftains became landlords if they had the favour of the English king, and clansmen became tenants who had to pay for the land they used.

A process began which became known as the 'Highland Clearances'. Many Scottish landlords destroyed individual small farms (known as 'crofts') to make space for large flocks of sheep and cattle. Evictions became very common in the early 19th century. Many Scottish people left for North America at this time.

> **Robert Burns (1759–96)**
> Known in Scotland as 'The Bard', Robert Burns was a Scottish poet. He wrote in the Scots language, English with some Scottish words, and standard English. He also revised a lot of traditional folk songs by changing or adding lyrics. Burns' best-known work is probably the song *Auld Lang Syne*, which is sung by people in the UK and other countries when they are celebrating the New Year (or Hogmanay in Scotland).

The Enlightenment

During the 18th century, new ideas about politics, philosophy and science were developed. This is often called 'the Enlightenment'. Many of the great thinkers of the Enlightenment were Scottish. Adam Smith developed ideas about economics which are still referred to today.

David Hume's ideas about human nature continue to influence philosophers. Scientific discoveries, such as James Watt's work on steam power, helped the progress of the Industrial Revolution.

One of the most important principles of the Enlightenment was that everyone should have the right to their own political and religious beliefs and that the state should not try to dictate to them. This continues to be an important principle in the UK today.

The Industrial Revolution

Before the 18th century, agriculture was the biggest source of employment in Britain. There were many cottage industries, where people worked from home to produce goods such as cloth and lace.

The Industrial Revolution was the rapid development of industry in Britain in the 18th and 19th centuries. Britain was the first country to industrialise on a large scale. It happened because of the development of machinery and the use of steam power. Agriculture and the manufacturing of goods became mechanised. This made things more efficient and increased production. Coal and other raw materials were needed to power the new factories. Many people moved from the countryside and started working in the mining and manufacturing industries.

The development of the Bessemer process for the mass production of steel led to the development of the shipbuilding industry and the railways. Manufacturing jobs became the main source of employment in Britain.

> **Richard Arkwright (1732–92)**
> Born in 1732, Arkwright originally trained and worked as a barber. He was able to dye hair and make wigs. When wigs became less popular, he started to work in textiles. He improved the original carding machine. Carding is the process of preparing fibres for spinning into yarn and fabric. He also developed horse-driven spinning mills that used only one machine. This increased the efficiency of production. Later, he used the steam engine to power machinery. Arkwright is particularly remembered for the efficient and profitable way that he ran his factories.

Better transport links were needed to transport raw materials and manufactured goods. Canals were built to link the factories to towns and cities and to the ports, particularly in the new industrial areas in the middle and north of England.

Working conditions during the Industrial Revolution were very poor. There were no laws to protect employees, who were often forced to work long hours in dangerous situations. Children also worked and were treated in the same way as adults. Sometimes they were treated even more harshly.

This was also a time of increased colonisation overseas. Captain James Cook mapped the coast of Australia and a few colonies were established there. Britain gained control over Canada, and the East India Company, originally set up to trade, gained control of large parts of India. Colonies began to be established in southern Africa.

Britain traded all over the world and began to import more goods. Sugar and tobacco came from North America and the West Indies; textiles, tea and spices came from India and the area that is today called Indonesia. Trading and settlements overseas sometimes brought Britain into conflict with other countries, particularly France, which was expanding and trading in a similar way in many of the same areas of the world.

> **Sake Dean Mahomet (1759–1851)**
> Mahomet was born in 1759 and grew up in the Bengal region of India. He served in the Bengal army and came to Britain in 1782. He then moved to Ireland and eloped with an Irish girl called Jane Daly in 1786, returning to England at the turn of the century. In 1810 he opened the Hindoostane Coffee House in George Street, London. It was the first curry house to open in Britain. Mahomet and his wife also introduced 'shampooing', the Indian art of head massage, to Britain.

The slave trade

This commercial expansion and prosperity was sustained in part by the booming slave trade. While slavery was illegal within Britain itself, by the 18th century it was a fully established overseas industry, dominated by Britain and the American colonies. Slaves came primarily from West Africa. Travelling on British ships in horrible conditions, they were taken to America and the Caribbean, where they were made to work on tobacco and sugar plantations. The living and working conditions for slaves were very bad. Many slaves tried to escape and others revolted against their owners in protest at their terrible treatment.

There were, however, people in Britain who opposed the slave trade. The first formal anti-slavery groups were set up by the Quakers in the late 1700s, and they petitioned Parliament to ban the practice. William Wilberforce, an evangelical Christian and a Member of Parliament, also played an important part in changing the law. Along with other abolitionists (people who supported the abolition of slavery), he succeeded in turning public opinion against the slave trade. In 1807, it became illegal to trade slaves in British ships or from British ports, and in 1833 the Emancipation Act abolished slavery throughout the British Empire. The Royal Navy stopped slave ships from other countries, freed the slaves and punished the slave traders. After 1833, 2 million Indian and Chinese workers were employed to replace the freed slaves. They worked on sugar plantations in the Caribbean, in mines in South Africa, on railways in East Africa and in the army in Kenya.

> *Slave trade became illegal in 1807 and slavery was abolished in 1833 by the Emancipation Act.*

The American war of independence

By the 1760s, there were substantial British colonies in North America. The colonies were wealthy and largely in control of their own affairs. Many of the colonist families had originally gone to North America in order to have religious freedom. They were well educated and interested in ideas of liberty. The British government wanted to tax the colonies. The colonists saw this as an attack on their freedom and said there should be 'no taxation without representation' in the British Parliament. Parliament tried to compromise by repealing some of the taxes, but relationships between the British government and the colonies continued to worsen.

Fighting broke out between the colonists and the British forces. In 1776, 13 American colonies declared their independence, stating that people had a right to establish their own governments. The colonists eventually defeated the British army and Britain recognised the colonies' independence in 1783.

War with France

During the 18th century, Britain fought a number of wars with France. In 1789, there was a revolution in France and the new French government soon declared war on Britain. Napoleon, who became Emperor of France, continued the war. Britain's navy fought against combined French and Spanish fleets, winning the Battle of Trafalgar in 1805.

Admiral Nelson was in charge of the British fleet at Trafalgar and was killed in the battle. Nelson's Column in Trafalgar Square, London, is a monument to him. His ship, HMS Victory, can be visited in Portsmouth. The British army also fought against the French. In 1815, the French Wars ended with the defeat of the Emperor Napoleon by the Duke of Wellington at the Battle of Waterloo. Wellington was known as the Iron Duke and later became Prime Minister.

The Union Flag

Although Ireland had had the same monarch as England and Wales since Henry VIII, it had remained a separate country. In 1801, Ireland became unified with England, Scotland and Wales after the Act of Union of 1800. This created the United Kingdom of Great Britain and Ireland. One symbol of this union between England, Scotland, Wales and Ireland was a new version of the official flag, the Union Flag. This is often called the Union Jack. The flag combined crosses associated with England, Scotland and Ireland. It is still used today as the official flag of the UK.

The Union Flag consists of three crosses:
- The cross of St George, patron saint of England, is a red cross on a white ground.
- The cross of St Andrew, patron saint of Scotland, is a diagonal white cross on a blue ground.
- The cross of St Patrick, patron saint of Ireland, is a diagonal red cross on a white ground.

There is also an official Welsh flag, which shows a Welsh dragon. The Welsh dragon does not appear on the Union Flag because, when the first Union Flag was created in 1606 from the flags of Scotland and England, the Principality of Wales was already united with England.

The Victorian Age

In 1837, Queen Victoria became queen of the UK at the age of 18. She reigned until 1901, almost 64 years. At the date of writing (2013) this is the longest reign of any British monarch. Her reign is known as the Victorian Age. It was a time when Britain increased in power and influence abroad. Within the UK, the middle classes because increasingly significant and a number of reformers led moves to improve conditions of life for the poor.

A long and illustrious history - A global power

The British Empire
During the Victorian period, the British Empire grew to cover all of India, Australia and large parts of Africa. It became the largest empire the world has ever seen, with an estimated population of more than 400 million people.

Many people were encouraged to leave the UK to settle overseas. Between 1853 and 1913, as many as 13 million British citizens left the country. People continued to come to Britain from other parts of the world. For example, between 1870 and 1914, around 120,000 Russian and Polish Jews came to Britain to escape persecution. Many settled in London's East End and in Manchester and Leeds. People from the Empire, including India and Africa, also came to Britain to live, work and study.

Trade and industry
Britain continued to be a great trading nation. The government began to promote policies of free trade, abolishing a number of taxes on imported goods. One example of this was the repealing of the Corn Laws in 1846. These had prevented the import of cheap grain. The reforms helped the development of British industry, because raw materials could now be imported more cheaply.

Working conditions in factories gradually became better. In 1847, the number of hours that women and children could work was limited by law to 10 hours per day. Better housing began to be built for workers.

Transport links also improved, enabling goods and people to move more easily around the country. Just before Victoria came to the throne, the father and son George and Robert Stephenson pioneered the railway engine and a major expansion of the railways took place in the Victorian period. Railways were built throughout the Empire. There were also great advances in other areas, such as the building of bridges by engineers such as Isambard Kingdom Brunel.

> **Isambard Kingdom Brunel (1806–59)**
> Brunel was originally from Portsmouth, England. He was an engineer who built tunnels, bridges, railway lines and ships. He was responsible for constructing the Great Western Railway, which was the first major railway built in Britain. It runs from Paddington Station in London to the south west of England, the West Midlands and Wales. Many of Brunel's bridges are still in use today.

British industry led the world in the 19th century. The UK produced more than half of the world's iron, coal and cotton cloth. The UK also became a centre for financial services, including insurance and banking. In 1851, the Great Exhibition opened in Hyde Park in the Crystal Palace, a huge building made of steel and glass. Exhibits ranged from huge machines to handmade goods. Countries from all over the world showed their goods but most of the objects were made in Britain.

The Crimean War

From 1853 to 1856, Britain fought with Turkey and France against Russia in the Crimean War. It was the first war to be extensively covered by the media through news stories and photographs. The conditions were very poor and many soldiers died from illnesses they caught in the hospitals, rather than from war wounds. Queen Victoria introduced the Victoria Cross medal during this war. It honours acts of valour by soldiers.

> **Florence Nightingale (1820–1910)**
> Florence Nightingale was born in Italy to English parents. At the age of 31, she trained as a nurse in Germany. In 1854, she went to Turkey and worked in military hospitals, treating soldiers who were fighting in the Crimean War. She and her fellow nurses improved the conditions in the hospital and reduced the mortality rate. In 1860 she established the Nightingale Training School for nurses at St Thomas' Hospital in London. The school was the first of its kind and still exists today, as do many of the practices that Florence used. She is often regarded as the founder of modern nursing.

Ireland in the 19th century

Conditions in Ireland were not as good as in the rest of the UK. Two-thirds of the population still depended on farming to make their living, often on very small plots of land. Many depended on potatoes as a large part of their diet. In the middle of the century the potato crop failed, and Ireland suffered a famine. A million people died from disease and starvation. Another million and a half left Ireland. Some emigrated to the United States and others came to England. By 1861 there were large populations of Irish people in cities such as Liverpool, London, Manchester and Glasgow.

The Irish Nationalist movement had grown strongly through the 19th century. Some, such as the Fenians, favoured complete independence. Others, such as Charles Stuart Parnell, advocated 'Home Rule', in which Ireland would remain in the UK but have its own parliament.

The right to vote

As the middle classes in the wealthy industrial towns and cities grew in influence, they began to demand more political power. The Reform Act of 1832 had greatly increased the number of people with the right to vote. The Act also abolished the old pocket and rotten boroughs (*see Constitutional Monarchy – The Bill of Rights p.25*) and more parliamentary seats were given to the towns and cities. There was a permanent shift of political power from the countryside to the towns but voting was still based on ownership of property. This meant that members of the working class were still unable to vote.

A movement began to demand the vote for the working classes and other people without property. Campaigners, called the Chartists, presented petitions to Parliament. At

> The Chartist campaigned from 1836 for workers right to vote, a salary for MPs, secret ballot, general elections and abolition of the need to own property

first they seemed to be unsuccessful, but in 1867 there was another Reform Act. This created many more urban seats in Parliament and reduced the amount of property that people needed to have before they could vote. However, the majority of men still did not have the right to vote and no women could vote.

Politicians realised that the increased number of voters meant that they needed to persuade people to vote for them if they were to be sure of being elected to Parliament. The political parties began to create organisations to reach out to ordinary voters. Universal suffrage (the right of every adult, male or female, to vote) followed in the next century.

In common with the rest of Europe, women in 19th century Britain had fewer rights than men. Until 1870, when a woman got married, her earnings, property and money automatically belonged to her husband. Acts of Parliament in 1870 and 1882 gave wives the right to keep their own earnings and property. In the late 19th and early 20th centuries, an increasing number of women campaigned and demonstrated for greater rights and, in particular, the right to vote. They formed the women's suffrage movement and became known as 'suffragettes'.

Emmeline Pankhurst (1858–1928)
Emmeline Pankhurst was born in Manchester in 1858. She set up the Women's Franchise League in 1889, which fought to get the vote in local elections for married women. In 1903 she helped found the Women's Social and Political Union (WSPU). This was the first group whose members were called 'suffragettes'. The group used civil disobedience as part of their protest to gain the vote for women. They chained themselves to railings, smashed windows and committed arson. Many of the women, including Emmeline, went on hunger strike. In 1918, women over the age of 30 were given voting rights and the right to stand for Parliament, partly in recognition of the contribution women made to the war effort during the First World War. Shortly before Emmeline's death in 1928, women were given the right to vote at the age of 21, the same as men.

The future of the Empire
Although the British Empire continued to grow until the 1920s, there was already discussion in the late 19th century about its future direction. Supporters of expansion believed that the Empire benefited Britain through increased trade and commerce. Others thought the

Empire had become over-expanded and that the frequent conflicts in many parts of the Empire, such as India's north-west frontier or southern Africa, were a drain on resources. Yet the great majority of British people believed in the Empire as a force for good in the world.

The Boer War of 1899 to 1902 made the discussions about the future of the Empire more urgent. The British went to war in South Africa with settlers from the Netherlands called the Boers. The Boers fought fiercely and the war went on for over three years. Many died in the fighting and many more from disease. There was some public sympathy for the Boers and people began to question whether the Empire could continue. As different parts of the Empire developed, they won greater freedom and autonomy from Britain. Eventually, by the second half of the 20th century, there was, for the most part, an orderly transition from Empire to Commonwealth, with countries being granted their independence.

The Boer War in South Africa (1899-1902) saw the start of a strong demand for independence by parts of the British empire.

Rudyard Kipling (1865–1936)
Rudyard Kipling was born in India in 1865 and later lived in India, the UK and the USA. He wrote books and poems set in both India and the UK. His poems and novels reflected the idea that the British Empire was a force for good. Kipling was awarded the Nobel Prize in Literature in 1907. His books include the Just So Stories and The Jungle Book, which continue to be popular today. His poem If has often been voted among the UK's favourite poems. It begins with these words:

'If you can keep your head when all about you
Are losing theirs and blaming it on you;
If you can trust yourself when all men doubt you,
But make allowance for their doubting too;
If you can wait and not be tired by waiting,
Or being lied about, don't deal in lies,
Or being hated, don't give way to hating,
And yet don't look too good, nor talk too wise'

(If, Rudyard Kipling)

The 20th century

The First World War

The early 20th century was a time of optimism in Britain. The nation, with its expansive Empire, well-admired navy, thriving industry and strong political institutions, was what is now known as a global 'superpower'. It was also a time of social progress. Financial help for the unemployed, old-age pensions and free school meals were just a few of the important measures introduced. Various laws were passed to improve safety in the workplace; town planning rules were tightened to prevent the further development of slums; and better support was given to mothers and their children after divorce or separation. Local government became more democratic and a salary for members of Parliament (MPs) was introduced for the first time, making it easier for more people to take part in public life.

This era of optimism and progress was cut short when war broke out between several European nations. On 28 June 1914, Archduke Franz Ferdinand of Austria was assassinated. This set off a chain of events leading to the First World War (1914–18). But while the assassination provided the trigger for war, other factors – such as a growing sense of nationalism in many European states; increasing militarism; imperialism; and the division of the major European powers into two camps – all set the conditions for war.

The conflict was centred in Europe, but it was a global war involving nations from around the world. Britain was part of the Allied Powers, which included (amongst others) France, Russia, Japan, Belgium, Serbia – and later, Greece, Italy, Romania and the United States. The whole of the British Empire was involved in the conflict – for example, more than a million Indians fought on behalf of Britain in lots of different countries, and around 40,000 were killed. Men from the West Indies, Africa, Australia, New Zealand and Canada also fought with the British. The Allies fought against the Central Powers – mainly Germany, the Austro-Hungarian Empire, the Ottoman Empire and later Bulgaria. Millions of people were killed or wounded, with more than 2 million British casualties. One battle, the British attack on the Somme in July 1916, resulted in about 60,000 British casualties on the first day alone.

The First World War ended at 11.00 am on 11th November 1918 with victory for Britain and its allies.

The partition of Ireland

In 1913, the British government promised 'Home Rule' for Ireland. The proposal was to have a self-governing Ireland with its own parliament but still part of the UK. A Home Rule Bill was introduced in Parliament. It was opposed by the Protestants in the north of Ireland, who threatened to resist Home Rule by force.

The outbreak of the First World War led the British government to postpone any changes in Ireland. Irish Nationalists were not willing to wait and in 1916 there was an uprising (the Easter Rising) against the British in Dublin. The leaders of the uprising were executed under military law. A guerrilla war against the British army and the police in Ireland followed. In 1921 a peace treaty was signed and in 1922 Ireland became two countries. The six counties in the north which were mainly Protestant remained part of the UK under the name Northern Ireland. The rest of Ireland became the Irish Free State. It had its own government and became a republic in 1949.

There were people in both parts of Ireland who disagreed with the split between the North and the South. They still wanted Ireland to be one independent country. Years of disagreement led to a terror campaign in Northern Ireland and elsewhere. The conflict between those wishing for full Irish independence and those wishing to remain loyal to the British government is often referred to as 'the Troubles'.

The inter-war period
In the 1920s, many people's living conditions got better. There were improvements in public housing and new homes were built in many towns and cities. However, in 1929, the world entered the 'Great Depression' and some parts of the UK suffered mass unemployment. The effects of the depression of the 1930s were felt differently in different parts of the UK. The traditional heavy industries such as shipbuilding were badly affected but new industries – including the automobile and aviation industries – developed. As prices generally fell, those in work had more money to spend. Car ownership doubled from 1 million to 2 million between 1930 and 1939. In addition, many new houses were built. It was also a time of cultural blossoming, with writers such as Graham Greene and Evelyn Waugh prominent. The economist John Maynard Keynes published influential new theories of economics. The BBC started radio broadcasts in 1922 and began the world's first regular television service in 1936.

The Second World War
Adolf Hitler came to power in Germany in 1933. He believed that the conditions imposed on Germany by the Allies after the First World War were unfair; he also wanted to conquer more land for the German people. He set about renegotiating treaties, building up arms, and testing Germany's military strength in nearby countries. The British government tried to avoid another war. However, when Hitler invaded Poland in 1939, Britain and France declared war in order to stop his aggression.

The war was initially fought between the Axis powers (fascist Germany and Italy and the Empire of Japan) and the Allies. The main countries on the allied side were the UK, France, Poland, Australia, New Zealand, Canada, and the Union of South Africa.

Having occupied Austria and invaded Czechoslovakia, Hitler followed his invasion of Poland by taking control of Belgium and the Netherlands. Then, in 1940, German forces defeated allied troops and advanced through France. At this time of national crisis, Winston Churchill became Prime Minister and Britain's war leader.

As France fell, the British decided to evacuate British and French soldiers from France in a huge naval operation. Many civilian volunteers in small pleasure and fishing boats from Britain helped the Navy to rescue more than 300,000 men from the beaches around Dunkirk. Although many lives and a lot of equipment were lost, the evacuation was a success and meant that Britain was better able to continue the fight against the Germans. The evacuation gave rise to the phrase 'the Dunkirk spirit'.

From the end of June 1940 until the German invasion of the Soviet Union in June 1941, Britain and the Empire stood almost alone against Nazi Germany.

Hitler wanted to invade Britain, but before sending in troops, Germany needed to control the air. The Germans waged an air campaign against Britain, but the British resisted with their fighter planes and eventually won the crucial aerial battle against the Germans, called 'the Battle of Britain', in the summer of 1940. The most important planes used by the Royal Air Force in the Battle of Britain were the Spitfire and the Hurricane – which were designed and built in Britain. Despite this crucial victory, the German air force was able to continue bombing London and other British cities at night-time. This was called the Blitz. Coventry was almost totally destroyed and a great deal of damage was done in other cities, especially in the East End of London. Despite the destruction, there was a strong national spirit of resistance in the UK. The phrase 'the Blitz spirit' is still used today to describe Britons pulling together in the face of adversity.

At the same time as defending Britain, the British military was fighting the Axis on many other fronts. In Singapore, the Japanese defeated the British and then occupied Burma, threatening India. The United States entered the war when the Japanese bombed its naval base at Pearl Harbour in December 1941.

That same year, Hitler attempted the largest invasion in history by attacking the Soviet Union. It was a fierce conflict, with huge losses on both sides. German forces were ultimately repelled by the Soviets, and the damage they sustained proved to be a pivotal point in the war.

The allied forces gradually gained the upper hand, winning significant victories in North Africa and Italy. German losses in the Soviet Union, combined with the support of the Americans, meant that the Allies were eventually strong enough to attack Hitler's forces in Western Europe. On 6 June 1944, allied forces landed in Normandy (this event is often referred to as 'D-Day'). Following victory on the beaches of Normandy, the allied forces pressed on through France and eventually into Germany. The Allies comprehensively defeated Germany in May 1945.

The war against Japan ended in August 1945 when the United States dropped its newly developed atom bombs on the Japanese cities of Hiroshima and Nagasaki. Scientists led by Ernest Rutherford, working at Manchester and then Cambridge University, were the first to 'split the atom' and took part in the Manhattan Project in the United States, which developed the atomic bomb. The war was finally over.

> **Winston Churchill (1874–1965)**
> Churchill was the son of a politician and, before becoming a Conservative MP in 1900, was a soldier and journalist. In May 1940 he became Prime Minister. He refused to surrender to the Nazis and was an inspirational leader to the British people in a time of great hardship. He lost the General Election in 1945 but returned as Prime Minister in 1951.
>
> He was an MP until he stood down at the 1964 General Election. Following his death in 1965, he was given a state funeral. He remains a much-admired figure to this day, and in 2002 was voted the greatest Briton of all time by the public. During the War, he made many famous speeches including lines which you may still hear:
>
> *'I have nothing to offer but blood, toil, tears and sweat'*
> Churchill's first PM speech to the House of Commons, 1940
>
> *'We shall fight on the beaches,*
> *we shall fight on the landing grounds,*
> *we shall fight in the fields and in the streets,*
> *we shall fight in the hills;*
> *we shall never surrender'*
> Speech to the House of Commons after Dunkirk (see above), 1940
>
> *'Never in the field of human conflict was so much owed by so many to so few'*
> Speech to the House of Commons during the Battle of Britain (see above), 1940

Britain since 1945

The welfare state

Although the UK had won the war, the country was exhausted economically and the people wanted change. During the war, there had been significant reforms to the education system and people now looked for wider social reforms.

In 1945 the British people elected a Labour government. The new Prime Minister was Clement Atlee, who promised to introduce the welfare state outlined in the Beveridge Report. In 1948, Aneurin (Nye) Bevan, the Minister for Health, led the establishment of the National Health Service (NHS), which guaranteed a minimum standard of health care for all, free at the point of use. A national system of benefits was also introduced to provide 'social security', so that the population would be protected from the 'cradle to the grave'. The government took into public ownership (nationalised) the railways, coal mines and gas, water and electricity supplies.

> **Alexander Fleming (1881–1955)**
> Born in Scotland, Fleming moved to London as a teenager and later qualified as a doctor. He was researching influenza (the 'flu') in 1928 when he discovered penicillin. This was then further developed into a usable drug by the scientists Howard Florey and Ernst Chain. By the 1940s it was in mass production. Fleming won the Nobel Prize in Medicine in 1945. Penicillin is still used to treat bacterial infections today.

Another aspect of change was self-government for former colonies. In 1947, independence was granted to nine countries, including India, Pakistan and Ceylon (now Sri Lanka). Other colonies in Africa, the Caribbean and the Pacific achieved independence over the next 20 years.

The UK developed its own atomic bomb and joined the new North Atlantic Treaty Organization (NATO), an alliance of nations set up to resist the perceived threat of invasion by the Soviet Union and its allies.

Britain had a Conservative government from 1951 to 1964. The 1950s were a period of economic recovery after the war and increasing prosperity for working people. The Prime Minister of the day, Harold Macmillan, was famous for his 'wind of change' speech about decolonisation and independence for the countries of the Empire.

> **Clement Attlee (1883–1967)**
> Clement Attlee was born in London in 1883. His father was a solicitor and, after studying at Oxford University, Attlee became a barrister. He gave this up to do social work in East London and eventually became a Labour MP. He was Winston Churchill's Deputy Prime Minister in the wartime coalition government and became Prime Minister after the Labour Party won the 1945 election. He was Prime Minister from 1945 to 1951 and led the Labour Party for 20 years. Attlee's government undertook the nationalisation of major industries (like coal and steel), created the National Health Service and implemented many of Beveridge's plans for a stronger welfare state. Attlee also introduced measures to improve the conditions of workers.

> **William Beveridge (1879–1963)**
> William Beveridge (later Lord Beveridge) was a British economist and social reformer. He served briefly as a Liberal MP and was subsequently the leader of the Liberals in the House of Lords but is best known for the 1942 report Social Insurance and Allied Services (known as the Beveridge Report). The report was commissioned by the wartime government in 1941. It recommended that the government should find ways of fighting the five 'Giant Evils' of Want, Disease, Ignorance, Squalor and Idleness and provided the basis of the modern welfare state.

A long and illustrious history - Britain since 1945

> **R A Butler (1902–82)**
> Richard Austen Butler (later Lord Butler) was born in 1902. He became a Conservative MP in 1923 and held several positions before becoming responsible for education in 1941. In this role, he oversaw the introduction of the Education Act 1944 (often called 'The Butler Act'), which introduced free secondary education in England and Wales. The education system has changed significantly since the Act was introduced, but the division between primary and secondary schools that it enforced still remains in most areas of Britain.

> **Dylan Thomas (1914–53)**
> Dylan Thomas was a Welsh poet and writer. He often read and performed his work in public, including for the BBC. His most well-known works include the radio play Under Milk Wood, first performed after his death in 1954, and the poem Do Not Go Gentle into That Good Night, which he wrote for his dying father in 1952. He died at the age of 39 in New York. There are several memorials to him in his birthplace, Swansea, including a statue and the Dylan Thomas Centre.

Migration in post-war Britain
Rebuilding Britain after the Second World War was a huge task. There were labour shortages and the British government encouraged workers from Ireland and other parts of Europe to come to the UK and help with the reconstruction. In 1948, people from the West Indies were also invited to come and work.

During the 1950s, there was still a shortage of labour in the UK. Further immigration was therefore encouraged for economic reasons, and many industries advertised for workers from overseas. For example, centres were set up in the West Indies to recruit people to drive buses. Textile and engineering firms from the north of England and the Midlands sent agents to India and Pakistan to find workers. For about 25 years, people from the West Indies, India, Pakistan and (later) Bangladesh travelled to work and settle in Britain.

Social change in the 1960s
The decade of the 1960s was a period of significant social change. It was known as 'the Swinging Sixties'. There was growth in British fashion, cinema and popular music. Two well-known pop music groups at the time were The Beatles and The Rolling Stones. People started to become better off and many bought cars and other consumer goods.

It was also a time when social laws were liberalised, for example in relation to divorce and to abortion in England, Wales and Scotland. The position of women in the workplace also improved. It was quite common at the time for employers to ask women to leave their jobs when they got married, but Parliament passed new laws giving women the right to equal pay and made it illegal for employers to discriminate against women because of their gender.

The 1960s was also a time of technological progress. Britain and France developed the world's only supersonic commercial airliner, Concorde. New styles of architecture, including high-rise buildings and the use of concrete and steel, became common.

The number of people migrating from the West Indies, India, Pakistan and what is now Bangladesh fell in the late 1960s because the government passed new laws to restrict immigration to Britain. Immigrants were required to have a strong connection to Britain through birth or ancestry. Even so, during the early 1970s, Britain admitted 28,000 people of Indian origin who had been forced to leave Uganda.

Some great British inventions of the 20th century

Britain has given the world some wonderful inventions. Examples from the 20th century include:

- The **television** was developed by Scotsman John Logie Baird (1888–1946) in the 1920s. In 1932 he made the first television broadcast between London and Glasgow.
- **Radar** was developed by Scotsman Sir Robert Watson-Watt (1892–1973), who proposed that enemy aircraft could be detected by radio waves. The first successful radar test took place in 1935.
- Working with radar led Sir Bernard Lovell (1913–2012) to make new discoveries in astronomy. The **radio telescope** he built at Jodrell Bank in Cheshire was for many years the biggest in the world and continues to operate today.
- A **Turing machine** is a theoretical mathematical device invented by Alan Turing (1912–54), a British mathematician, in the 1930s. The theory was influential in the development of computer science and the modern-day computer.
- The Scottish physician and researcher John MacLeod (1876–1935) was the co-discoverer of **insulin**, used to treat diabetes.
- The **structure of the DNA molecule** was discovered in 1953 through work at British universities in London and Cambridge. This discovery contributed to many scientific advances, particularly in medicine and fighting crime. Francis Crick (1916–2004), one of those awarded the Nobel Prize for this discovery, was British.
- The **jet engine** was developed in Britain in the 1930s by Sir Frank Whittle (1907–96), a British Royal Air Force engineer Officer.
- Sir Christopher Cockerell (1910–99), a British inventor, invented the **hovercraft** in the 1950s.
- Britain and France developed **Concorde**, the world's only supersonic passenger aircraft. It first flew in 1969 and began carrying passengers in 1976. Concorde was retired from service in 2003.
- The **Harrier jump jet**, an aircraft capable of taking off vertically, was also designed and developed in the UK.

- In the 1960s, James Goodfellow (1937–) invented the **cash-dispensing ATM** (automatic teller machine) or 'cashpoint'. The first of these was put into use by Barclays Bank in Enfield, north London in 1967.
- **IVF (in-vitro fertilisation) therapy** for the treatment of infertility was pioneered in Britain by physiologist Sir Robert Edwards (1925–) and gynaecologist Patrick Steptoe (1913–88). The world's first 'test-tube baby' was born in Oldham, Lancashire in 1978.
- In 1996, two British scientists, Sir Ian Wilmot (1944–) and Keith Campbell (1954–2012), led a team which was the first to succeed in **cloning a mammal**, Dolly the sheep. This has led to further research into the possible use of cloning to preserve endangered species and for medical purposes.
- Sir Peter Mansfield (1933–), a British scientist, is the co-inventor of the **MRI (magnetic resonance imaging) scanner**. This enables doctors and researchers to obtain exact and non-invasive images of human internal organs and has revolutionised diagnostic medicine.
- The inventor of the **World Wide Web**, Sir Tim Berners-Lee (1955–), is British. Information was successfully transferred via the web for the first time on 25 December 1990.

Problems in the economy in the 1970s

In the late 1970s, the post-war economic boom came to an end. Prices of goods and raw materials began to rise sharply and the exchange rate between the pound and other currencies was unstable. This caused problems with the 'balance of payments': imports of goods were valued at more than the price paid for exports.

Many industries and services were affected by strikes and this caused problems between the trade unions and the government. People began to argue that the unions were too powerful and that their activities were harming the UK.

The 1970s were also a time of serious unrest in Northern Ireland. In 1972, the Northern Ireland Parliament was suspended and Northern Ireland was directly ruled by the UK government. Some 3,000 people lost their lives in the decades after 1969 in the violence in Northern Ireland.

> **Mary Peters (1939–)**
> Born in Manchester, Mary Peters moved to Northern Ireland as a child. She was a talented athlete who won an Olympic gold medal in the pentathlon in 1972. After this, she raised money for local athletics and became the team manager for the women's British Olympic team. She continues to promote sport and tourism in Northern Ireland and was made a Dame of the British Empire in 2000 in recognition of her work.

Europe and the Common Market

West Germany, France, Belgium, Italy, Luxembourg and the Netherlands formed the European Economic Community (EEC) in 1957. At first the UK did not wish to join the EEC but it eventually did so in 1973. The UK has been since a full member of the European Union but does not use the Euro currency.

In June 2016, and by way of a referendum, the UK has chosen to leave the European Union and will likely do so during 2019.

> **Roald Dahl (1916–1990)**
> Roald Dahl was born in Wales to Norwegian parents. He served in the Royal Air Force during the Second World War. It was during the 1940s that he began to publish books and short stories. He is most well known for his children's books, although he also wrote for adults. His best-known works include Charlie and the Chocolate Factory and George's Marvellous Medicine. Several of his books have been made into films.

Conservative government from 1979 to1997

Margaret Thatcher, Britain's first woman Prime Minister, led the Conservative government from 1979 to 1990. The government made structural changes to the economy through the privatisation of nationalised industries and imposed legal controls on trade union powers.

Deregulation saw a great increase in the role of the City of London as an international centre for investments, insurance and other financial services. Traditional industries, such as shipbuilding and coal mining, declined. In 1982, Argentina invaded the Falkland Islands, a British overseas territory in the South Atlantic. A naval taskforce was sent from the UK and military action led to the recovery of the islands. John Major was Prime Minister after Mrs Thatcher, and helped establish the Northern Ireland peace process.

> **Margaret Thatcher (1925–2013)**
> Margaret Thatcher was the daughter of a grocer from Grantham in Lincolnshire. She trained as a chemist and lawyer. She was elected as a Conservative MP in 1959 and became a cabinet minister in 1970 as the Secretary of State for Education and Science. In 1975 she was elected as Leader of the Conservative Party and so became Leader of the Opposition. Following the Conservative victory in the General Election in 1979, Margaret Thatcher became the first woman Prime Minister of the UK. She was the longest-serving Prime Minister of the 20th century, remaining in Office until 1990. During her premiership, there were a number of important economic reforms within the UK. She worked closely with the United States President, Ronald Reagan, and was one of the first Western leaders to recognise and welcome the changes in the leadership of the Soviet Union which eventually led to the end of the Cold War.

Labour government from 1997-2010

In 1997 the Labour Party led by Tony Blair was elected. The Blair government introduced a Scottish Parliament and a Welsh Assembly (see Devolved Administrations). The Scottish Parliament has substantial powers to legislate. The Welsh Assembly was given fewer legislative powers but considerable control over public services. In Northern Ireland, the Blair government was able to build on the peace process, resulting in the Good Friday Agreement signed in 1998. The Northern Ireland Assembly was elected in 1999 but suspended in 2002. It was not reinstated until 2007. Most paramilitary groups in Northern Ireland have decommissioned their arms and are inactive. Gordon Brown took over as Prime Minister in 2007.

Conflicts in Afghanistan and Iraq

Throughout the 1990s, Britain played a leading role in coalition forces involved in the liberation of Kuwait, following the Iraqi invasion in 1990, and the conflict in the Former Republic of Yugoslavia. Since 2000, British armed forces have been engaged in the global fight against international terrorism and against the proliferation of weapons of mass destruction, including operations in Afghanistan and Iraq. British combat troops left Iraq in 2009. The UK now operates in Afghanistan as part of the United Nations (UN) mandated 50-nation International Security Assistance Force

(ISAF) coalition and at the invitation of the Afghan government. ISAF is working to ensure that Afghan territory can never again be used as a safe haven for international terrorism, where groups such as Al Qa'ida could plan attacks on the international community. As part of this, ISAF is building up the Afghan National Security Forces and is helping to create a secure environment in which governance and development can be extended. International forces are gradually handing over responsibility for security to the Afghans, who will have full security responsibility in all provinces by the end of 2014.

Coalition government from 2010-2015

In May 2010, and for the first time in the UK since February 1974, no political party won an overall majority in the General Election. The Conservative and Liberal Democrat parties formed a coalition and the leader of the Conservative Party, David Cameron, became Prime Minister.

Conservative Government from 2015 onward

In the General Elections of 2015, the Conservative party won an outright majority and David Cameron remained Prime Minister, but this time formed a fully Conservative government.

The EU referendum of 2016 and the aftermath

During the campaign of 2015, David Cameron made a pledge to renegotiate British membership of the European Union (EU). In 2016, a referendum took place, called the Brexit referendum in a contraction of the words Britain and exit. The result was 51.6% votes in favour of leaving the European Union. Having been in favour of the remaining option throughout, David Cameron resigned and was succeeded by Theresa May on July 2016.

Theresa May organised a new General Election in 2017. The Conservative won, but narrowly after Theresa May secured the support of the Democratic Unionist Party (DUP) from Northern Ireland.

Negotiations to leave the European Union have been ongoing since 2016 and are likely to conclude in 2019.

2019 change of Prime Minister

The Prime minister, Theresa May, announced on May 24th 2019 that she would resign as leader of the Conservative Party on June 7th. This triggered a leadership contest within the party. The next leader would also become Prime Minister.

Through a series of ballots, the MPs reduced the list of 10 candidates to only 2: Boris Johnson and Jeremy Hunt.

The choice was put to the vote of all members of the Conservative Party.

Boris Johnson won. On July 24th, the Queen accepted Theresa May's resignation as Prime Minister and appointed Boris Johnson to the role.

He has promised the UK would leave the European Union on October 31st.

A long and illustrious history

Test your knowledge

1. Who was Henry VII?
   A. The leader of the House of York
   B. The leader of the House of Lancaster
   C. The leader of the House of Buckingham
   D. The leader of the House of Leeds

2. What British discovery was influential in the development of computer science and the modern-day computer?
   A. The Radar
   B. The Turing machine
   C. The MRI scanner
   D. The aeroplane

3. During the Middle Ages, a Parliament was developed in Scotland, which had three Houses called Estates. These were:
   A. The lords, the commons and the clergy
   B. The lords, the commons and the farmers
   C. The farmers, the blacksmiths and the clergy
   D. The farmers, the blacksmiths and the teachers

4. Which of the following was one of the most famous battles of the Hundred Years War?
   A. The Battle of Agincourt
   B. The Battle of Bannockburn
   C. The Battle of Culloden
   D. The Battle of Waterloo

5. What is the meaning of the term 'Habeas corpus'?
   A. You must present the person in court
   B. You must obey the law
   C. You should go to court
   D. You should not be judged

A long and illustrious history

6. Which of the following events relates to the German bombing of London and other cities at night time during the World War II?
- A. The Bombing
- B. The German raid
- C. The Blitz
- D. The Axis

7. Which was the first major railway built in Britain?
- A. High Speed 1
- B. West Coast Main Line
- C. Great Western Railway
- D. East London Line

8. Who was the leader of the English Republic?
- A. King Richard III
- B. Oliver Cromwell
- C. Charles II
- D. Charles I

9. When did the Vikings first visit Britain to raid coastal towns and take away goods and slaves?
- A. AD 600
- B. AD 790
- C. AD 789
- D. AD 804

10. Who was the first person to lead a Roman invasion in Britain in 55 BC?
- A. Napoleon
- B. Emperor Claudius
- C. William Caxton
- D. Julius Caesar

Answers: 1.B - 2.B - 3.A - 4.A - 5.A - 6.C - 7.C - 8.B - 9.C - 10.D

A MODERN, THRIVING SOCIETY

In this chapter you will learn about the population and culture of the UK. The start of the chapter shows you where the major cities of the UK are. You should be sure you can identify the various cities, such as Leeds and Bradford, confidently. Because the UK is a multicultural country you will also have to know the sizes of the different ethnic and religious groups in the UK, as well as their main festivals.
The chapter focuses on British culture .

Make sure that you know and understand:
- who each of the people described are and what they have achieved,
- Britain's sporting success and general information about sport in the UK,
- the poems, films, books and other works listed,
- the artists, composers, architects, authors, poets and other famous people.
- the extracts of poems provided,
- the famous landmarks at the end of the chapter.

The UK today

The UK today is a more diverse society than it was 100 years ago, in both ethnic and religious terms. Post-war immigration means that nearly 10% of the population has a parent or grandparent born outside the UK. The UK continues to be a multinational and multiracial society with a rich and varied culture. This section will tell you about the different parts of the UK and some of the important places. It will also explain some of the UK's traditions, customs and some of the popular activities that take place.

The nations of the UK
The UK is located in the north west of Europe. The longest distance on the mainland is from John O'Groats on the north coast of Scotland to Land's End in the south-west corner of England. It is about 870 miles (approximately 1,400 kilometres). Most people live in towns and cities but much of Britain is still countryside. Many people continue to visit the countryside for holidays and for leisure activities such as walking, camping and fishing.

The United Kingdom is formed of four countries:	
England	Northern Ireland
Wales	Scotland

Cities of the UK

ENGLAND
- London
- Birmingham
- Liverpool
- Leeds
- Sheffield
- Bristol
- Manchester
- Bradford
- Newcastle Upon Tyne
- Plymouth
- Southampton
- Norwich

WALES
- Cardiff
- Swansea
- Newport

SCOTLAND
- Edinburgh
- Glasgow
- Dundee
- Aberdeen

NORTHERN IRELAND
- Belfast

The Capital Cities of the UK:

England	London
Northern Ireland	Belfast
Wales	Cardiff
Scotland	Edinburgh

UK currency

The currency in the UK is the pound sterling (symbol £). There are 100 pence in a pound.

The denominations (values) of currency are:
coins: 1p, 2p, 5p, 10p, 20p, 50p, £1 and £2
notes: £5, £10, £20, £50.

Northern Ireland and Scotland have their own banknotes, which are valid everywhere in the UK. However, shops and businesses do not have to accept them.

Languages and dialects

There are many variations in language in the different parts of the UK. The English language has many accents and dialects. In Wales, many people speak Welsh – a completely different language from English – and it is taught in schools and universities. In Scotland, Gaelic (again, a different language) is spoken in some parts of the Highlands and Islands, and in Northern Ireland some people speak Irish Gaelic.

In Scotland, Gaelic is spoken in some parts of the Highlands and Islands, and in Northern Ireland some people speak Irish Gaelic.

An ageing population

People in the UK are living longer than ever before. This is due to improved living standards and better health care. There are now a record number of people aged 85 and over. This has an impact on the cost of pensions and health care.

Population growth has been faster in more recent years. Migration into the UK and longer life expectancy have played a part in population growth.

The population is very unequally distributed over the four parts of the UK. England more or less consistently makes up 84% of the total population, Wales around 5%, Scotland just over 8% and Northern Ireland less than 3%.

Ethnic diversity

The UK population is ethnically diverse and changing rapidly, especially in large cities such as London. It is not always easy to get an exact picture of the ethnic origin of all the population. There are people in the UK with ethnic origins from all over the world. In surveys, the most common ethnic description chosen is white, which includes people of European, Australian, Canadian, New Zealand and American descent. Other significant groups are those of Asian, black and mixed descent.

An equal society

Within the UK, it is a legal requirement that men and women should not be discriminated against because of their gender or because they are, or are not, married. They have equal rights to work, own property, marry and divorce. If they are married, both parents are equally responsible for their children.

Women in Britain today make up about half of the workforce. On average, girls leave school with better qualifications than boys. More women than men study at university.

Employment opportunities for women are much greater than they were in the past. Women work in all sectors of the economy, and there are now more women in high-level positions than ever before, including senior managers in traditionally male-dominated occupations. Alongside this, men now work in more varied jobs than they did in the past.

It is no longer expected that women should stay at home and not work. Women often continue to work after having children. In many families today, both partners work and both share responsibility for childcare and household chores.

Religion

The UK is historically a Christian country. In the 2009 Citizenship Survey, 70% of people identified themselves as Christian. Much smaller proportions identified themselves as Muslim (4%), Hindu (2%), Sikh (1%), Jewish or Buddhist (both less than 0.5%), and 2% of people followed another religion. There are religious buildings for other religions all over the UK. This includes Islamic mosques, Hindu temples, Jewish synagogues, Sikh gurdwaras and Buddhist temples. However, everyone has the legal right to choose their religion, or to choose not to practise a religion. In the Citizenship Survey, 21% of people said that they had no religion.

Christian Churches
In England, there is a constitutional link between Church and state. The official Church of the state is the Church of England (called the Anglican Church in other countries and the Episcopal Church in Scotland and the United States). It is a Protestant Church and has existed since the Reformation in the 1530s (see Religious Conflicts for an explanation).

The monarch is the head of the Church of England. The spiritual leader of the Church of England is the Archbishop of Canterbury. The monarch has the right to select the Archbishop and other senior church officials, but usually the choice is made by the Prime Minister and a committee appointed by the Church. Several Church of England bishops sit in the House of Lords (see House of Lords).

In Scotland, the national Church is the Church of Scotland, which is a Presbyterian Church. It is governed by ministers and elders. The chairperson of the General Assembly of the Church of Scotland is the Moderator, who is appointed for one year only and often speaks on behalf of that Church.

There is no established Church in Wales or Northern Ireland. Other Protestant Christian groups in the UK are Baptists, Methodists, Presbyterians and Quakers. There are also other denominations of Christianity, the biggest of which is Roman Catholic.

Patron Saints' days
England, Scotland, Wales and Northern Ireland each have a national saint, called a patron saint.

Each country of the UK has a Saint and a Special day		
England	23 April	St George
Northern Ireland	17 March	St Patrick
Wales	1 March	St David
Scotland	30 November	St Andrew

Only Scotland and Northern Ireland have their patron saint's day as an official holiday (although in Scotland not all businesses and Offices will close). Events are held across Scotland, Northern Ireland and the rest of the country, especially where there are a lot of people of Scottish, Northern Irish and Irish heritage.

While the patron saints' days are no longer public holidays in England and Wales, they are still celebrated. Parades and small festivals are held all over the two countries.

A modern, thriving society - Customs and traditions

Customs and traditions

The main Christian festivals

Christmas Day, 25 December, celebrates the birth of Jesus Christ. It is a public holiday. Many Christians go to church on Christmas Eve (24 December) or on Christmas Day itself. Christmas is celebrated in a traditional way. People usually spend the day at home and eat a special meal, which often includes roast turkey, Christmas pudding and mince pies. They give gifts, send cards and decorate their houses. Christmas is a special time for children. Very young children believe that Father Christmas (also known as Santa Claus) brings them presents during the night before Christmas Day. Many people decorate a tree in their home. Boxing Day is the day after Christmas Day and is a public holiday.

Easter takes place in March or April. It marks the death of Jesus Christ on Good Friday and his rising from the dead on Easter Sunday. Both Good Friday and the following Monday, called Easter Monday, are public holidays.

The 40 days before Easter are known as Lent. It is a time when Christians take time to reflect and prepare for Easter. Traditionally, people would fast during this period and today many people will give something up, like a favourite food. The day before Lent starts is called Shrove Tuesday, or Pancake Day. People eat pancakes, which were traditionally made to use up foods such as eggs, fat and milk before fasting. Lent begins on Ash Wednesday. There are church services where Christians are marked with an ash cross on their forehead as a symbol of death and sorrow for sin.

Easter is also celebrated by people who are not religious. 'Easter eggs' are chocolate eggs often given as presents at Easter as a symbol of new life.

Shrove Tuesday	Day before Lent
Ash Wednesday	Start of Lent
Lent	40 days before Easter
Easter Sunday	Sunday following first full moon after 20 March
Christmas Eve	24 December
Christmas Day	25 December
Boxing Day	26 December

Other religious festivals

- Diwali normally falls in October or November and lasts for five days. It is often called the Festival of Lights. It is celebrated by Hindus and Sikhs. It celebrates the victory of good over evil and the gaining of knowledge. There are different stories about how the festival came about. There is a famous celebration of Diwali in Leicester.
- Hannukah is in November or December and is celebrated for eight days. It is to remember the Jews' struggle for religious freedom. On each day of the festival a candle is lit on a stand of eight candles (called a menorah) to remember the story of the festival, where oil that should have lasted only a day did so for eight.

A modern, thriving society - Customs and traditions

- Eid al-Fitr celebrates the end of Ramadan, when Muslims have fasted for a month. They thank Allah for giving them the strength to complete the fast. The date when it takes place changes every year. Muslims attend special services and meals.
- Eid ul Adha remembers that the prophet Ibrahim was willing to sacrifice his son when God ordered him to. It reminds Muslims of their own commitment to God. Many Muslims sacrifice an animal to eat during this festival. In Britain this has to be done in a slaughterhouse.
- Vaisakhi (also spelled Baisakhi) is a Sikh festival which celebrates the founding of the Sikh community known as the Khalsa. It is celebrated on 14 April each year with parades, dancing and singing.

Diwali	Hindus and Sikhs	5 days in October or November
Hanukah	Jews	8 days in November or December
Eid al-Fitr	Muslims	end of Ramadan
Eid ul Adha	Muslims	10th day of last Islamic month
Vaisakhi	Sikhs	14 April

Other festivals and traditions
- **New Year**, 1 January, is a public holiday. People usually celebrate on the night of 31 December (called New Year's Eve). In Scotland, 31 December is called Hogmanay and 2 January is also a public holiday. For some Scottish people, Hogmanay is a bigger holiday than Christmas.
- **Valentine's Day**, 14 February, is when lovers exchange cards and gifts. Sometimes people send anonymous cards to someone they secretly admire.
- **April Fool's Day**, 1 April, is a day when people play jokes on each other until midday. The television and newspapers often have stories that are April Fool jokes.
- **Mothering Sunday (or Mother's Day)** is the Sunday three weeks before Easter. Children send cards or buy gifts for their mothers.
- **Father's Day** is the third Sunday in June. Children send cards or buy gifts for their fathers.
- **Halloween**, 31 October, is an ancient festival and has roots in the pagan festival to mark the beginning of winter. Young people will often dress up in frightening costumes to play 'trick or treat'. People give them treats to stop them playing tricks on them. A lot of people carve lanterns out of pumpkins and put a candle inside.
- **Bonfire Night**, 5 November, is an occasion when people in Great Britain set off fireworks at home or in special displays. The origin of this celebration was an event in 1605, when a group of Catholics led by Guy Fawkes failed in their plan to kill the Protestant king with a bomb in the Houses of Parliament.
- **Remembrance Day**, 11 November, commemorates those who died fighting for the UK and its allies. Originally it commemorated the dead of the First World War, which ended on 11 November 1918. People wear poppies (the red flower found on the

battlefields of the First World War). At 11.00 am there is a two-minute silence and wreaths are laid at the Cenotaph in Whitehall, London.

Bank holidays

As well as those mentioned previously, there are other public holidays each year called bank holidays, when banks and many other businesses are closed for the day. These are of no religious significance. They are at the beginning of May, in late May or early June, and in August. In Northern Ireland, the anniversary of the Battle of the Boyne in July is also a public holiday.

January, 1	New Year
February, 14	Valentine's Day
April, 1	April Fool's Day
Sunday, 3 weeks before Easter	Mother's Day
1st Monday of May	Bank Holiday
Last Monday of May	Bank Holiday
3rd Sunday in June	Father's Day
Last Monday of August	Bank Holiday
October, 1	Halloween
November, 5	Bonfire Night
November, 11	Remembrance Day
December, 24	Christmas Eve
December, 25	Christmas Day
December, 26	Boxing Day

Sport

Sports of all kinds play an important part in many people's lives. There are several sports that are particularly popular in the UK. Many sporting events take place at major stadiums such as Wembley Stadium in London and the Millennium Stadium in Cardiff.

Local governments and private companies provide sports facilities such as swimming pools, tennis courts, football pitches, dry ski slopes and gymnasiums. Many famous sports, including cricket, football, lawn tennis, golf and rugby, began in Britain.

The UK has hosted the Olympic Games on three occasions: 1908, 1948 and 2012. The main Olympic site for the 2012 Games was in Stratford, East London. The British team was very successful, across a wide range of Olympic sports, finishing third in the medal table.

The Paralympic Games for 2012 were also hosted in London. The Paralympics have their origin in the work of Dr Sir Ludwig Guttman, a German refugee, at the Stoke Mandeville hospital in Buckinghamshire. Dr Guttman developed new methods of treatment for people with spinal injuries and encouraged patients to take part in exercise and sport.

Notable British sportsmen and women
- **Sir Roger Bannister** (1929–2018) was the first man in the world to run a mile in under four minutes, in 1954.
- **Sir Jackie Stewart** (1939–) is a Scottish former racing driver who won the Formula 1 world championship three times.
- **Bobby Moore** (1941–93) captained the English football team that won the World Cup in 1966.
- **Sir Ian Botham** (1955–) captained the English cricket team and holds a number of English Test cricket records, both for batting and for bowling.
- **Jayne Torvill** (1957–) and Christopher Dean (1958–) won gold medals for ice dancing at the Olympic Games in 1984 and in four consecutive world championships.
- **Sir Steve Redgrave** (1962–) won gold medals in rowing in five consecutive Olympic Games and is one of Britain's greatest Olympians.
- **Baroness Tanni-Grey Thompson** (1969–) is an athlete who uses a wheelchair and won 16 Paralympic medals, including 11 gold medals, in races over five Paralympic Games. She won the London Marathon six times and broke a total of 30 world records.
- **Dame Kelly Holmes** (1970–) won two gold medals for running in the 2004 Olympic Games. She has held a number of British and European records.
- **Dame Ellen MacArthur** (1976–) is a yachtswoman and in 2004 became the fastest person to sail around the world singlehanded.
- **Sir Chris Hoy** (1976–) is a Scottish cyclist who has won six gold and one silver Olympic medals. He has also won 11 world championship titles.
- **David Weir** (1979–) is a Paralympian who uses a wheelchair and has won six gold medals over two Paralympic Games. He has also won the London Marathon six times.
- **Bradley Wiggins** (1980–) is a cyclist. In 2012, he became the first Briton to win the Tour de France. He has won seven Olympic medals, including gold medals in the 2004, 2008 and 2012 Olympic Games.
- **Mo Farah** (1983–) is a British distance runner, born in Somalia. He won gold medals in the 2012 Olympics for the 5,000 and 10,000 metres and is the first Briton to win the Olympic gold medal in the 10,000 metres.
- **Jessica Ennis** (1986–) is an athlete. She won the 2012 Olympic gold medal in the heptathlon, which includes seven different track and field events. She also holds a number of British athletics records.
- **Andy Murray** (1987–) is a Scottish tennis player who in 2012 won the men's singles in the US Open. He is the first British man to win a singles title in a Grand Slam tournament since 1936. In the same year, he won Olympic gold and silver medals and was runner-up in the men's singles at Wimbledon (see Tennis).
- **Ellie Simmonds** (1994–) is a Paralympian who won gold medals for swimming at the 2008 and 2012 Paralympic Games and holds a number of world records. She was the youngest member of the British team at the 2008 Games.

Cricket

Cricket originated in England and is now played in many countries. Games can last up to five days but still result in a draw! The idiosyncratic nature of the game and its complex laws are said to reflect the best of the British character and sense of fair play. You may come across expressions such as 'rain stopped play', 'batting on a sticky wicket', 'playing a straight bat', 'bowled a googly' or 'it's just not cricket', which have passed into everyday usage. The most famous competition is the Ashes, which is a series of Test matches played between England and Australia.

Football

Football is the UK's most popular sport. It has a long history in the UK and the first professional football clubs were formed in the late 19th century.

England, Scotland, Wales and Northern Ireland each have separate leagues in which clubs representing different towns and cities compete. The English Premier League attracts a huge international audience. Many of the best players in the world play in the Premier League. Many UK teams also compete in competitions such as the UEFA (Union of European Football Associations) Champions League, against other teams from Europe. Most towns and cities have a professional club and people take great pride in supporting their home team. There can be great rivalry between different football clubs and among fans.

Each country in the UK also has its own national team that competes with other national teams across the world in tournaments such as the FIFA (Fédération Internationale de Football Association) World Cup and the UEFA European Football Championships. England's only international tournament victory was at the World Cup of 1966, hosted in the UK.

Football is also a popular sport to play in many local communities, with people playing amateur games every week in parks all over the UK.

Rugby

Rugby originated in England in the early 19th century and is very popular in the UK today. There are two different types of rugby, which have different rules: union and league. Both have separate leagues and national teams in England, Wales, Scotland and Northern Ireland (who play with the Irish Republic). Teams from all countries compete in a range of competitions. The most famous rugby union competition is the Six Nations Championship between England, Ireland, Scotland, Wales, France and Italy. The Super League is the most well-known rugby league (club) competition.

Horse-racing

There is a very long history of horse racing in Britain, with evidence of events taking place as far back as Roman times. The sport has a long association with royalty. There are racecourses all over the UK. Famous horse-racing events include: Royal Ascot, a five-day race meeting in Berkshire attended by members of the Royal Family; the Grand National at Aintree near Liverpool; and the Scottish Grand National at Ayr. There is a National Horseracing Museum in Newmarket, Suffolk.

Golf

The modern game of golf can be traced back to 15th century Scotland. It is a popular sport played socially as well as professionally. There are public and private golf courses all over the UK. St Andrews in Scotland is known as the home of golf. The Open Championship is the only 'Major' tournament held outside the United States. It is hosted by a different golf course every year.

Tennis

Modern tennis evolved in England in the late 19th century. The first tennis club was founded in Leamington Spa in 1872. The most famous tournament hosted in Britain is The Wimbledon Championships, which takes place each year at the All England Lawn Tennis and Croquet Club. It is the oldest tennis tournament in the world and the only 'Grand Slam' event played on grass.

Water sports

Sailing continues to be popular in the UK, reflecting our maritime heritage. A British sailor, Sir Francis Chichester, was the first person to sail single-handed around the world, in 1966/67. Two years later, Sir Robin Knox-Johnston became the first person to do this without stopping. Many sailing events are held throughout the UK, the most famous of which is at Cowes on the Isle of Wight. Rowing is also popular, both as a leisure activity and as a competitive sport. There is a popular yearly race on the Thames between Oxford and Cambridge Universities.

Motor sports

There is a long history of motor sport in the UK, for both cars and motor cycles. Motor-car racing in the UK started in 1902. The UK continues to be a world leader in the development and manufacture of motor-sport technology. A Formula 1 Grand Prix event is held in the UK each year and a number of British Grand Prix drivers have won the Formula 1 World Championship. Recent British winners include Damon Hill, Lewis Hamilton and Jensen Button.

Skiing

Skiing is increasingly popular in the UK. Many people go abroad to ski and there are also dry ski slopes throughout the UK. Skiing on snow may also be possible during the winter. There are five ski centres in Scotland, as well as Europe's longest dry ski slope near Edinburgh.

Arts and culture

Music

Music is an important part of British culture, with a rich and varied heritage. It ranges from classical music to modern pop. There are many different venues and musical events that take place across the UK.

The Proms is an eight-week summer season of orchestral classical music that takes place in various venues, including the Royal Albert Hall in London. It has been organised by the British Broadcasting Corporation (BBC) since 1927. The Last Night of the Proms is the most well-known concert and (along with others in the series) is broadcast on television.

Classical music has been popular in the UK for many centuries. **Henry Purcell** (1659–95) was the organist at Westminster Abbey. He wrote church music, operas and other pieces, and developed a British style distinct from that elsewhere in Europe. He continues to be influential on British composers.

The German-born composer **George Frederick Handel** (1695–1759) spent many years in the UK and became a British citizen in 1727. He wrote the Water Music for King George I and Music for the Royal Fireworks for his son, George II. Both these pieces continue to be very popular. Handel also wrote an oratorio, Messiah, which is sung regularly by choirs, often at Easter time.

More recently, important composers include **Gustav Holst** (1874–1934), whose work includes The Planets, a suite of pieces themed around the planets of the solar system. He adapted Jupiter, part of the Planets suite, as the tune for I vow to thee my country, a popular hymn in British churches.

Sir Edward Elgar (1857–1934) was born in Worcester, England. His best-known work is probably the Pomp and Circumstance Marches. March No 1 (Land of Hope and Glory) is usually played at the Last Night of the Proms at the Royal Albert Hall.

Ralph Vaughan Williams (1872–1958) wrote music for orchestras and choirs. He was strongly influenced by traditional English folk music.

Sir William Walton (1902–83) wrote a wide range of music, from film scores to opera. He wrote marches for the coronations of King George VI and Queen Elizabeth II but his best-known works are probably Façade, which became a ballet, and Balthazar's Feast, which is intended to be sung by a large choir.

Benjamin Britten (1913–76) is best known for his operas, which include Peter Grimes and Billy Budd. He also wrote A Young Person's Guide to the Orchestra, which is based on a piece of music by Purcell and introduces the listener to the various different sections of an orchestra. He founded the Aldeburgh festival in Suffolk, which continues to be a popular music event of international importance.

Other types of popular music, including folk music, jazz, pop and music, have flourished in Britain since the 20th century. Britain has had an impact on popular music around the world, due to the wide use of the English language, the UK's cultural links with many countries, and British capacity for invention and innovation. Since the 1960s, British pop music has made one of the most important cultural contributions to life in the UK. Bands including The Beatles and The Rolling Stones continue to have an influence on music both here and abroad. British pop music has continued to innovate – for example, the Punk movement of the late 1970s, and the trend towards boy and girl bands in the 1990s.

There are many large venues that host music events throughout the year, such as: Wembley Stadium; The O2 in Greenwich, south-east London; and the Scottish Exhibition and Conference Centre (SECC) in Glasgow.

Festival season takes place across the UK every summer, with major events in various locations. Famous festivals include Glastonbury, the Isle of Wight Festival and the V Festival. Many bands and solo artists, both well-known and up-and-coming, perform at these events.

The National Eisteddfod of Wales is an annual cultural festival which includes music, dance, art and original performances largely in Welsh. It includes a number of important competitions for Welsh poetry.

The Mercury Music Prize is awarded each September for the best album from the UK and Ireland. The Brit Awards is an annual event that gives awards in a range of categories, such as best British group and best British solo artist.

Theatre
There are theatres in most towns and cities throughout the UK, ranging from the large to the small. They are an important part of local communities and often show both professional and amateur productions. London's West End, also known as 'Theatreland', is particularly well known. The Mousetrap, a murder-mystery play by Dame Agatha Christie, has been running in the West End since 1952 and has had the longest initial run of any show in history.

There is also a strong tradition of musical theatre in the UK. In the 19th century, Gilbert and Sullivan wrote comic operas, often making fun of popular culture and politics. These operas include HMS Pinafore, The Pirates of Penzance and The Mikado. Gilbert and Sullivan's work is still often staged by professional and amateur groups. More recently, Andrew Lloyd Webber has written the music for shows which have been popular throughout the world, including, in collaboration with Tim Rice, Jesus Christ Superstar and Evita, and also Cats and The Phantom of the Opera.

One British tradition is the pantomime. Many theatres produce a pantomime at Christmas time. They are based on fairy stories and are light-hearted plays with music and comedy, enjoyed by family audiences. One of the traditional characters is the Dame, a woman played by a man. There is often also a pantomime horse or cow played by two actors in the same costume.

A modern, thriving society - Arts and culture

The Edinburgh Festival takes place in Edinburgh, Scotland, every summer. It is a series of different arts and cultural festivals, with the biggest and most well-known being the Edinburgh Festival Fringe ('the Fringe'). The Fringe is a showcase of mainly theatre and comedy performances. It often shows experimental work.

The Laurence Olivier Awards take place annually at different venues in London. There are a variety of categories, including best director, best actor and best actress. The awards are named after the British actor Sir Laurence Olivier, later Lord Olivier, who was best known for his roles in various Shakespeare plays.

Art

During the Middle Ages, most art had a religious theme, particularly wall paintings in churches and illustrations in religious books. Much of this was lost after the Protestant Reformation but wealthy families began to collect other paintings and sculptures. Many of the painters working in Britain in the 16th and 17th centuries were from abroad – for example, Hans Holbein and Sir Anthony Van Dyck. British artists, particularly those painting portraits and landscapes, became well known from the 18th century onwards.

Works by British and international artists are displayed in galleries across the UK. Some of the most well-known galleries are The National Gallery, Tate Britain and Tate Modern in London, the National Museum in Cardiff, and the National Gallery of Scotland in Edinburgh.

The Turner Prize was established in 1984 and celebrates contemporary art. It was named after Joseph Turner. Four works are shortlisted every year and shown at Tate Britain before the winner is announced. The Turner Prize is recognised as one of the most prestigious visual art awards in Europe. Previous winners include Damien Hirst and Richard Wright.

Notable British artists
- **Thomas Gainsborough** (1727–88) was a portrait painter who often painted people in country or garden scenery.
- **David Allan** (1744–96) was a Scottish painter who was best known for painting portraits. One of his most famous works is called The Origin of Painting.
- **Joseph Turner** (1775–1851) was an influential landscape painter in a modern style. He is considered the artist who raised the profile of landscape painting.
- **John Constable** (1776–1837) was a landscape painter most famous for his works of Dedham Vale on the Suffolk–Essex border in the east of England.
- The Pre-Raphaelites were an important group of artists in the second half of the 19th century. They painted detailed pictures on religious or literary themes in bright colours. They included **Holman Hunt**, **Dante Gabriel Rossetti** and **Sir John Millais**.
- **Sir John Lavery** (1856–1941) was a very successful Northern Irish portrait painter. His work included painting the Royal Family.
- **Henry Moore** (1898–1986) was an English sculptor and artist. He is best known for his large bronze abstract sculptures.

- **John Petts** (1914–91) was a Welsh artist, best known for his engravings and stained glass.
- **Lucian Freud** (1922–2011) was a German-born British artist. He is best known for his portraits.
- **David Hockney** (1937–) was an important contributor to the 'pop art' movement of the 1960s and continues to be influential today.

Architecture

The architectural heritage of the UK is rich and varied. In the Middle Ages, great cathedrals and churches were built, many of which still stand today. Examples are the cathedrals in Durham, Lincoln, Canterbury and Salisbury. The White Tower in the Tower of London is an example of a Norman castle keep, built on the orders of William the Conqueror (see The Norman Conquest and The Tower of London).

Gradually, as the countryside became more peaceful and landowners became richer, the houses of the wealthy became more elaborate and great country houses such as Hardwick Hall in Derbyshire were built. British styles of architecture began to evolve.

In the 17th century, Inigo Jones took inspiration from classical architecture to design the Queen's House at Greenwich and the Banqueting House in Whitehall in London. Later in the century, Sir Christopher Wren helped develop a British version of the ornate styles popular in Europe in buildings such as the new St Paul's Cathedral.

In the 18th century, simpler designs became popular. The Scottish architect Robert Adam influenced the development of architecture in the UK, Europe and America. He designed the inside decoration as well as the building itself in great houses such as Dumfries House in Scotland. His ideas influenced architects in cities such as Bath, where the Royal Crescent was built.

In the 19th century, the medieval 'gothic' style became popular again. As cities expanded, many great public buildings were built in this style. The Houses of Parliament and St Pancras Station were built at this time, as were the town halls in cities such as Manchester and Sheffield.

In the 20th century, Sir Edwin Lutyens had an influence throughout the British Empire. He designed New Delhi to be the seat of government in India. After the First World War, he was responsible for many war memorials throughout the world, including the Cenotaph in Whitehall. The Cenotaph is the site of the annual Remembrance Day service attended by the Queen, politicians and foreign ambassadors (see The Cenotaph).

Modern British architects including Sir Norman Foster, Lord (Richard) Rogers and Dame Zaha Hadid continue to work on major projects throughout the world as well as within the UK.

Alongside the development of architecture, garden design and landscaping have played an important role in the UK. In the 18th century, Lancelot 'Capability' Brown designed the grounds around country houses so that the landscape appeared to be natural, with grass, trees and lakes. He often said that a place had 'capabilities'. Later, Gertrude Jekyll often worked with Edwin Lutyens to design colourful gardens around the houses he designed. Gardens continue to be an important part of homes in the UK. The annual Chelsea Flower Show showcases garden design from Britain and around the world.

Fashion and design
Britain has produced many great designers, from Thomas Chippendale (who designed furniture in the 18th century) to Clarice Cliff (who designed Art Deco ceramics) to Sir Terence Conran (a 20th-century interior designer). Leading fashion designers of recent years include Mary Quant, Alexander McQueen and Vivienne Westwood.

Literature
The UK has a prestigious literary history and tradition. Several British writers, including the novelist Sir William Golding, the poet Seamus Heaney, and the playwright Harold Pinter, have won the Nobel Prize in Literature. Other authors have become well known in popular fiction. Agatha Christie's detective stories are read all over the world and Ian Fleming's books introduced James Bond. In 2003, The Lord of the Rings by JRR Tolkien was voted the country's best-loved novel.

The Man Booker Prize for Fiction is awarded annually for the best fiction novel written by an author from the Commonwealth, Ireland or Zimbabwe. It has been awarded since 1968. Past winners include Ian McEwan, Hilary Mantel and Julian Barnes.

Notable authors and writers
- **Jane Austen** (1775–1817) was an English novelist. Her books include Pride and Prejudice and Sense and Sensibility. Her novels are concerned with marriage and family relationships. Many have been made into television programmes or films.
- **Charles Dickens** (1812–70) wrote a number of very famous novels, including Oliver Twist and Great Expectations. You will hear references in everyday talk to some of the characters in his books, such as Scrooge (a mean person) or Mr Micawber (always hopeful).
- **Robert Louis Stevenson** (1850–94) wrote books which are still read by adults and children today. His most famous books include Treasure Island, Kidnapped and Dr Jekyll and Mr Hyde.
- **Thomas Hardy** (1840–1928) was an author and poet. His best-known novels focus on rural society and include Far from the Madding Crowd and Jude the Obscure.
- **Sir Arthur Conan Doyle** (1859–1930) was a Scottish doctor and writer. He was best known for his stories about Sherlock Holmes, who was one of the first fictional detectives.
- **Evelyn Waugh** (1903–66) wrote satirical novels, including Decline and Fall and Scoop. He is perhaps best known for Brideshead Revisited.
- **Sir Kingsley Amis** (1922–95) was an English novelist and poet. He wrote more than 20 novels. The most well-known is Lucky Jim.

- **Graham Green**e (1904–91) wrote novels often influenced by his religious beliefs, including The Heart of the Matter, The Honorary Consul, Brighton Rock and Our Man in Havana.
- **J K Rowling** (1965–) wrote the Harry Potter series of children's books, which have enjoyed huge international success. She now writes fiction for adults as well.

British poets

British poetry is among the richest in the world. The Anglo-Saxon poem Beowulf tells of its hero's battles against monsters and is still translated into modern English. Poems which survive from the Middle Ages include Chaucer's Canterbury Tales and a poem called Sir Gawain and the Green Knight, about one of the knights at the court of King Arthur.

As well as plays, Shakespeare wrote many sonnets (poems which must be 14 lines long) and some longer poems. As Protestant ideas spread, a number of poets wrote poems inspired by their religious views. One of these was John Milton, who wrote Paradise Lost.

Other poets, including William Wordsworth, were inspired by nature. Sir Walter Scott wrote poems inspired by Scotland and the traditional stories and songs from the area on the borders of Scotland and England. He also wrote novels, many of which were set in Scotland.

Poetry was very popular in the 19th century, with poets such as William Blake, John Keats, Lord Byron, Percy Shelley, Alfred Lord Tennyson, and Robert and Elizabeth Browning. Later, many poets – for example, Wilfred Owen and Siegfried Sassoon – were inspired to write about their experiences in the First World War. More recently, popular poets have included Sir Walter de la Mare, John Masefield, Sir John Betjeman and Ted Hughes. Some of the best-known poets are buried or commemorated in Poet's Corner in Westminster Abbey.

Some famous lines include:

'Oh to be in England now that April's there
And whoever wakes in England sees, some morning, unaware,
That the lowest boughs and the brushwood sheaf
Round the elm-tree bole are in tiny leaf
While the Chaffinch sings on the orchard bough
In England – Now!'
(Robert Browning, 1812–89 – Home Thoughts from Abroad)
'She walks in beauty, like the night
Of cloudless climes and starry skies,
All that's best of dark and bright
Meet in her aspect and her eyes'
(Lord Byron, 1788–1824 – She Walks in Beauty)

'I wander'd lonely as a cloud
That floats on high o'er vales and hills
When all at once I saw a crowd,
A host of golden daffodils'
(William Wordsworth, 1770–1850 – The Daffodils)

'Tyger! Tyger! Burning bright
In the forests of the night,
What immortal hand or eye
Could frame thy fearful symmetry?'
(William Blake, 1757–1827 – The Tyger)

'What passing-bells for these who die as cattle?
Only the monstrous anger of the guns.
Only the stuttering rifles' rapid rattle
Can patter out their hasty orisons.'
(Wilfred Owen, 1893–1918 – Anthem for Doomed Youth)

Leisure

People in the UK spend their leisure time in many different ways.

Gardening

A lot of people have gardens at home and will spend their free time looking after them. Some people rent additional land called 'an allotment', where they grow fruit and vegetables. Gardening and flower shows range from major national exhibitions to small local events. Many towns have garden centres selling plants and gardening equipment. There are famous gardens to visit throughout the UK, including Kew Gardens, Sissinghurst and Hidcote in England, Crathes Castle and Inveraray Castle in Scotland, Bodnant Garden in Wales, and Mount Stewart in Northern Ireland.

The countries that make up the UK all have flowers which are particularly associated with them and which are sometimes worn on national saints' days.

England - Rose   N.Ireland - Shamrock   Wales - Daffodil   Scotland - Thistle

Shopping

There are many different places to go shopping in the UK. Most towns and cities have a central shopping area, which is called the town centre. Undercover shopping centres are also common – these might be in town centres or on the outskirts of a town or city. Most shops in the UK are open seven days a week, although trading hours on Sundays and public holidays are generally reduced. Many towns also have markets on one or more days a week, where stallholders sell a variety of goods.

Cooking and food

Many people in the UK enjoy cooking. They often invite each other to their homes for dinner. A wide variety of food is eaten in the UK because of the country's rich cultural heritage and diverse population.

Traditional foods

There are a variety of foods that are traditionally associated with different parts of the UK:
- **England**: Roast beef, which is served with potatoes, vegetables, Yorkshire puddings (batter that is baked in the oven) and other accompaniments. Fish and chips are also popular.
- **Wales**: Welsh cakes – a traditional Welsh snack made from flour, dried fruits and spices, and served either hot or cold.
- **Scotland**: Haggis – a sheep's stomach stuffed with offal, suet, onions and oatmeal.
- **Northern Ireland**: Ulster fry – a fried meal with bacon, eggs, sausage, black pudding, white pudding, tomatoes, mushrooms, soda bread and potato bread.

Films - British film industry

Films were first shown publicly in the UK in 1896 and film screenings very quickly became popular. From the beginning, film makers became famous for clever special effects and this continues to be an area of British expertise. From the early days of the cinema, British actors have worked in both the UK and USA. Sir Charles (Charlie) Chaplin became famous in silent movies for his tramp character and was one of many British actors to make a career in Hollywood.

British studios flourished in the 1930s. Eminent directors included Sir Alexander Korda and Sir Alfred Hitchcock, who later left for Hollywood and remained an important film director until his death in 1980. During the Second World War, British movies (for example, In Which We Serve) played an important part in boosting morale. Later, British directors including Sir David Lean and Ridley Scott found great success both in the UK and internationally.

The 1950s and 1960s were a high point for British comedies, including Passport to Pimlico, The Ladykillers and, later, the Carry On films.

Many of the films now produced in the UK are made by foreign companies, using British expertise. Some of the most commercially successful films of all time, including the two highest-grossing film franchises (Harry Potter and James Bond), have been produced in the UK. Ealing Studios has a claim to being the oldest continuously working film studio facility in the world. Britain continues to be particularly strong in special effects and animation. One example is the work of Nick Park, who has won four Oscars for his animated films, including three for films featuring Wallace and Gromit.

Actors such as Sir Lawrence Olivier, David Niven, Sir Rex Harrison and Richard Burton starred in a wide variety of popular films. British actors continue to be popular and continue to win awards throughout the world. Recent British actors to have won Oscars include .
The annual British Academy Film Awards, hosted by the British Academy of Film and Television Arts (BAFTA), are the British equivalent of the Oscars.

Oscar winners: Colin Firth, Sir Anthony Hopkins, Dame Judi Dench, Kate Winslet and Tilda Swinton

Some famous British films
- **The 39 Steps** (1935), directed by Alfred Hitchcock
- **Brief Encounter** (1945), directed by David Lean
- **The Third Man** (1949), directed by Carol Reed
- **The Belles of St Trinian's** (1954), directed by Frank Launder
- **Lawrence of Arabia** (1962), directed by David Lean
- **Women in Love** (1969), directed by Ken Russell
- **Don't Look Now** (1973), directed by Nicolas Roeg
- **Chariots of Fire** (1981), directed by Hugh Hudson
- **The Killing Fields** (1984), directed by Roland Joffé
- **Four Weddings and a Funeral** (1994), directed by Mike Newell
- **Touching the Void** (2003), directed by Kevin MacDonald.

British comedy
The traditions of comedy and satire, and the ability to laugh at ourselves, are an important part of the UK character. Medieval kings and rich nobles had jesters who told jokes and made fun of people in the Court. Later, Shakespeare included comic characters in his plays. In the 18th century, political cartoons attacking prominent politicians – and, sometimes, the monarch or other members of the Royal Family – became increasingly popular. In the 19th century, satirical magazines began to be published. The most famous was Punch, which was published for the first time in the 1840s. Today, political cartoons continue to be published in newspapers, and magazines such as Private Eye continue the tradition of satire.

Comedians were a popular feature of British music hall, a form of variety theatre which was very common until television became the leading form of entertainment in the UK. Some of the people who had performed in the music halls in the 1940s and 1950s, such as Morecambe and Wise, became stars of television.

Television comedy developed its own style. Situation comedies, or sitcoms, which often look at family life and relationships in the workplace, remain popular. Satire has also continued to be important, with shows like That Was The Week That Was in the 1960s and Spitting Image in the 1980s and 1990s. In 1969, Monty Python's Flying Circus introduced a new type of progressive comedy. Stand-up comedy, where a solo comedian talks to a live audience, has become popular again in recent years.

Television and radio
Many different television (TV) channels are available in the UK. Some are free to watch and others require a paid subscription. British television shows a wide variety of programmes. Popular programmes include regular soap operas such as Coronation Street and EastEnders. In Scotland, some Scotland-specific programmes are shown and there is also a channel with programmes in the Gaelic language. There is a Welsh-language channel in Wales. There are also programmes specific to Northern Ireland and some programmes broadcast in Irish Gaelic.

Everyone in the UK with a TV, computer or other medium which can be used for watching TV must have a television licence. One licence covers all of the equipment in one home, except when people rent different rooms in a shared house and each has a separate tenancy agreement – those people must each buy a separate licence. People over 75 can apply for a free TV licence and blind people can get a 50% discount. You will receive a fine of up to £1,000 if you watch TV but do not have a TV licence.

The money from TV licences is used to pay for the British Broadcasting Corporation (BBC). This is a British public service broadcaster providing television and radio programmes. The BBC is the largest broadcaster in the world. It is the only wholly state-funded media organisation that is independent of government. Other UK channels are primarily funded through advertisements and subscriptions.

There are also many different radio stations in the UK. Some broadcast nationally and others in certain cities or regions. There are radio stations that play certain types of music and some broadcast in regional languages such as Welsh or Gaelic. Like television, BBC radio stations are funded by TV licences and other radio stations are funded through advertisements.

Social networking
Social networking websites such as Facebook and Twitter are a popular way for people to stay in touch with friends, organise social events, and share photos, videos and opinions. Many people use social networking on their mobile phones when out and about.

Pubs and night clubs
Public houses (pubs) are an important part of the UK social culture. Many people enjoy meeting friends in the pub. Most communities will have a 'local' pub that is a natural focal point for social activities. Pub quizzes are popular. Pool and darts are traditional pub

games. To buy alcohol in a pub or night club you must be 18 or over, but people under that age may be allowed in some pubs with an adult. When they are 16, people can drink wine or beer with a meal in a hotel or restaurant (including eating areas in pubs) as long as they are with someone over 18.

Pubs are usually open during the day from 11.00 am (12 noon on Sundays). Night clubs with dancing and music usually open and close later than pubs. The licensee decides the hours that the pub or night club is open.

Betting and gambling
In the UK, people often enjoy a gamble on sports or other events. There are also casinos in many places. You have to be 18 to go into betting shops or gambling clubs. There is a National Lottery for which draws are made every week. You can enter by buying a ticket or a scratch card. People under 16 are not allowed to participate in the National Lottery.
Pets
A lot of people in the UK have pets such as cats or dogs. They might have them for company or because they enjoy looking after them. It is against the law to treat a pet cruelly or to neglect it. All dogs in public places must wear a collar showing the name and address of the owner. The owner is responsible for keeping the dog under control and for cleaning up after the animal in a public place.

Vaccinations and medical treatment for animals are available from veterinary surgeons (vets). There are charities which may help people who cannot afford to pay a vet.

Places of interest

The UK has a large network of public footpaths in the countryside. There are also many opportunities for mountain biking, mountaineering and hill walking. There are 15 national parks in England, Wales and Scotland. They are areas of protected countryside that everyone can visit, and where people live, work and look after the landscape.

There are many museums in the UK, which range from small community museums to large national and civic collections. Famous landmarks exist in towns, cities and the countryside throughout the UK. Most of them are open to the public to view (generally for a charge).

Many parts of the countryside and places of interest are kept open by the National Trust in England, Wales and Northern Ireland and the National Trust for Scotland. Both are charities that work to preserve important buildings, coastline and countryside in the UK. The National Trust was founded in 1895 by three volunteers. There are now more than 61,000 volunteers helping to keep the organisation running.

A modern, thriving society - Places of interest

UK landmarks

Big Ben is the nickname for the great bell of the clock at the Houses of Parliament in London. Many people call the clock Big Ben as well. The clock is over 150 years old and is a popular tourist attraction. The clock tower is named 'Elizabeth Tower' in honour of Queen Elizabeth II's Diamond Jubilee in 2012.

A modern, thriving society - Places of interest

The Eden Project is located in Cornwall, in the south west of England. Its biomes, which are like giant greenhouses, house plants from all over the world. The Eden Project is also a charity which runs environmental and social projects internationally.

Edinburgh Castle is a dominant feature of the skyline in Scotland. It has a long history, dating back to the early Middle Ages. It is looked after by Historic Scotland, a Scottish government agency.

A modern, thriving society - Places of interest

Located on the north-east coast of Northern Ireland, **the Giant's Causeway** is a land formation of columns made from volcanic lava. It was formed about 50 million years ago. There are many legends about the Causeway and how it was formed.

Loch Lomond and the Trossachs National Park. This national park covers 720 square miles (1,865 square kilometres) in the west of Scotland. Loch Lomond is the largest expanse of fresh water in mainland Britain and probably the best-known part of the park.

A modern, thriving society - Places of interest

The London Eye is situated on the southern bank of the River Thames and is a Ferris wheel that is 443 feet (135 metres) tall. It was originally built as part of the UK's celebration of the new millennium and continues to be an important part of New Year celebrations.

Snowdonia is a national park in North Wales. It covers an area of 838 square miles (2,170 square kilometres). Its most well-known landmark is Snowdon, which is the highest mountain in Wales.

A modern, thriving society - Places of interest

The Tower of London was first built by William the Conqueror after he became king in 1066. Tours are given by the Yeoman Warders, also known as Beefeaters, who tell visitors about the building's history. People can also see the Crown Jewels there.

The Lake District is England's largest national park. It covers 885 square miles (2,292 square kilometres). It is famous for its lakes and mountains and is very popular with climbers, walkers and sailors. The biggest stretch of water is Windermere. In 2007, television viewers voted Wastwater as Britain's favourite view.

A modern, thriving society

Test your knowledge

1. Which famous poem tells the story of the knights at the court of King Arthur?
A. Beowulf
B. Paradise Lost
C. Sir Gawain and the Green Knight
D. King Arthur and his knights

2. Light-hearted plays with music and comedy, which are enjoyed by family audiences and based on fairy stories are known as:
A. Children's plays
B. Pantomimes
C. Hogmanay
D. Parades

3. What is the minimum age requirement in the UK for people to be able to drink wine or beer with a meal in a hotel or restaurant as long as they are with someone over 18?
A. 14 years old
B. 15 years old
C. 16 years old
D. 17 years old

4. Which of the following landmarks is the largest expanse of fresh water in mainland Britain?
A. The River Thames
B. Loch Lomond
C. Loch Ness
D. Lake District

5. Who led the group of Catholics who tried to kill the Protestant king with a bomb in the Houses of the Parliament in 1605?
A. Oliver Cromwell
B. Alexander II
C. Guy Fawkes
D. Adrian IV

A modern, thriving society

6. Who wrote an oratorio called 'Messiah', which is regularly sung by choirs at Easter time?
A. George Frederick Handel
B. Sir Edward Elgar
C. Gustav Holst
D. Henry Purcell

7. What is the most well-known rugby league (club) competition?
A. The Grand National
B. The All England championship
C. The Six Nations championship
D. The Super League

8. Which of the following British poets was inspired by nature?
A. Geoffrey Chaucer
B. William Blake
C. Sir Walter Scott
D. William Wordsworth

9. Where does the most famous sailing event in the UK take place?
A. Holyhead, in North Wales
B. Cowes, in the Isle of Wight
C. Douglas, in the Isle of Man
D. Plymouth, in the South West of England

10. Which TWO British areas have their own banknotes?
A. Northern Ireland
B. Scotland
C. Wales
D. The Isle of Man

Answers: 1.C - 2.B - 3.C - 4.B - 5.C - 6.A - 7.D - 8.D - 9.B - 10.A,B

THE UK GOVERNMENT, THE LAW AND YOUR ROLE

In this chapter you will learn how the UK is governed. You need to understand the Queen's role in government and her powers. Make sure you understand how people are appointed to the two Houses of Parliament and the specific roles detailed, such as the Speaker and cabinet, and your rights to vote and stand for election. Everyone should understand the workings of the devolved administrations but pay particular attention if you are taking the test in Scotland, Wales or Northern Ireland.

Make sure you know and understand:
- The UK's international role,
- the Commonwealth, EU and other bodies and their member countries,
- common laws, fundamental rights, policing,
- the differences between the various courts and offences,
- taxation, driving and community activity,
- the UK's parliamentary democracy with the monarch as head of state,
- the different institutions which make up this democratie,
- how you can play a part in the democratic process.

The development of British democracy

Democracy is a system of government where the whole adult population gets a say. This might be by direct voting or by choosing representatives to make decisions on their behalf. At the turn of the 19th century, Britain was not a democracy as we know it today. Although there were elections to select members of Parliament (MPs), only a small group of people could vote. They were men who were over 21 years of age and who owned a certain amount of property.

The franchise (that is, the number of people who had the right to vote) grew over the course of the 19th century and political parties began to involve ordinary men and women as members.

In the 1830s and 1840s, a group called the Chartists campaigned for reform. They wanted six changes:
- for every man to have the vote
- elections every year
- for all regions to be equal in the electoral system
- secret ballots
- for any man to be able to stand as an MP
- for MPs to be paid.

81

At the time, the campaign was generally seen as a failure. However, by 1918 most of these reforms had been adopted. The voting franchise was also extended to women over 30, and then in 1928 to men and women over 21. In 1969, the voting age was reduced to 18 for men and women.

The British constitution

A constitution is a set of principles by which a country is governed. It includes all of the institutions that are responsible for running the country and how their power is kept in check. The constitution also includes laws and conventions. The British constitution is not written down in any single document, and therefore it is described as 'unwritten'. This is mainly because the UK, unlike America or France, has never had a revolution which led permanently to a totally new system of government. Our most important institutions have developed over hundreds of years. Some people believe that there should be a single document, but others believe an unwritten constitution allows for more flexibility and better government.

Constitutional institutions
In the UK, there are several different parts of government. The main ones are:

- the monarchy
- Parliament (the House of Commons and the House of Lords)
- the Prime Minister
- the cabinet
- the judiciary (courts)
- the police
- the civil service
- local government.

In addition, there are devolved governments in Scotland, Wales and Northern Ireland that have the power to legislate on certain issues.

The monarchy
Queen Elizabeth II is the head of state of the UK. She is also the monarch or head of state for many countries in the Commonwealth. The UK has a constitutional monarchy. This means that the king or queen does not rule the country but appoints the government, which the people have chosen in a democratic election. The monarch invites the leader of the party with the largest number of MPs, or the leader of a coalition between more than one party, to become the Prime Minister. The monarch has regular meetings with

the Prime Minister and can advise, warn and encourage, but the decisions on government policies are made by the Prime Minister and cabinet (see The government).

The Queen has reigned since her father's death in 1952, and in 2012 she celebrated her Diamond Jubilee (60 years as queen). She is married to Prince Philip, the Duke of Edinburgh. Her eldest son, Prince Charles (the Prince of Wales), is the heir to the throne.

The Queen has important ceremonial roles, such as the opening of the new parliamentary session each year. On this occasion the Queen makes a speech which summarises the government's policies for the year ahead. All Acts of Parliament are made in her name.

The Queen represents the UK to the rest of the world. She receives foreign ambassadors and high commissioners, entertains visiting heads of state, and makes state visits overseas in support of diplomatic and economic relationships with other countries.

The Queen has an important role in providing stability and continuity. While governments and Prime Ministers change regularly, the Queen continues as head of state. She provides a focus for national identity and pride, which was demonstrated through the celebrations of her Jubilee.

The National Anthem

The National Anthem of the UK is 'God Save the Queen'. It is played at important national occasions and at events attended by the Queen or the Royal Family. The first verse is:

'God save our gracious Queen!
Long live our noble Queen!
God save the Queen!
Send her victorious,
Happy and glorious,
Long to reign over us,
God save the Queen!'

New citizens swear or affirm loyalty to the Queen as part of the citizenship ceremony.

Oath of allegiance

'I (name) swear by Almighty God that on becoming a British citizen, I will be faithful and bear true allegiance to Her Majesty Queen Elizabeth the Second, her Heirs and Successors, according to law.'

Affirmation of allegiance

'I (name) do solemnly, sincerely and truly declare and affirm that on becoming a British citizen, I will be faithful and bear true allegiance to Her Majesty Queen Elizabeth the Second, her Heirs and Successors, according to law.'

System of government

The system of government in the UK is a parliamentary democracy. The UK is divided into parliamentary constituencies. Voters in each constituency elect their member of Parliament (MP) in a General Election. All of the elected MPs form the House of Commons. Most MPs belong to a political party, and the party with the majority of MPs forms the government. If one party does not get a majority, two parties can join together to form a coalition.

The House of Commons

The House of Commons is regarded as the more important of the two chambers in Parliament because its members are democratically elected. The Prime Minister and almost all the members of the cabinet are members of the House of Commons (MPs). Each MP represents a parliamentary constituency, which is a small area of the country. MPs have a number of different responsibilities. They:

- represent everyone in their constituency
- help to create new laws
- scrutinise and comment on what the government is doing
- debate important national issues.

The House of Lords

Members of the House of Lords, known as peers, are not elected by the people and do not represent a constituency. The role and membership of the House of Lords has changed over the last 50 years.
Until 1958, all peers were:

- 'hereditary', which means they inherited their title, or
- senior judges, or
- bishops of the Church of England.

Since 1958, the Prime Minister has had the power to nominate peers just for their own lifetime. These are called life peers. They have usually had an important career in politics, business, law or another profession. Life peers are appointed by the monarch on the advice of the Prime Minister. They also include people nominated by the leaders of the other main political parties or by an independent Appointments Commission for non-party peers.

Since 1999, hereditary peers have lost the automatic right to attend the House of Lords. They now elect a few of their number to represent them in the House of Lords.

The House of Lords is normally more independent of the government than the House of Commons. It can suggest amendments or propose new laws, which are then discussed by MPs. The House of Lords checks laws that have been passed by the House of Commons to ensure they are fit for purpose. It also holds the government to account to make sure that it is working in the best interests of the people. There are peers who are specialists in particular areas, and their knowledge is useful in making and checking laws. The House of Commons has powers to overrule the House of Lords, but these are not used often.

The Speaker

Debates in the House of Commons are chaired by the Speaker. This person is the chief Officer of the House of Commons. The Speaker is neutral and does not represent a political party, even though he or she is an MP, represents a constituency and deals with constituents' problems like any other MP. The Speaker is chosen by other MPs in a secret ballot.

The Speaker keeps order during political debates to make sure the rules are followed. This includes making sure the opposition (see The government) has a guaranteed amount of time to debate issues which it chooses. The Speaker also represents Parliament on ceremonial occasions.

Elections

UK elections

MPs are elected at a General Election, which is held at least every five years.

If an MP dies or resigns, there will be a fresh election, called a byelection, in his or her constituency.

MPs are elected through a system called 'first past the post'. In each constituency, the candidate who gets the most votes is elected. The government is usually formed by the party that wins the majority of constituencies. If no party wins a majority, two parties may join together to form a coalition.

European parliamentary elections

Elections for the European Parliament are also held every five years. Elected members are called members of the European Parliament (MEPs). Elections to the European Parliament use a system of proportional representation, where seats are allocated to each party in proportion to the total number of votes it has won.

Contacting elected members

All elected members have a duty to serve and represent their constituents. You can get contact details for all your representatives and their parties from your local library and from www.parliament.uk. MPs, Assembly members, members of the Scottish Parliament (MSPs) and MEPs are also listed in The Phone Book, published by BT, and in Yellow Pages. You can contact MPs by letter or telephone at their constituency Office, or at their Office in the House of Commons: The House of Commons, Westminster, London SW1A 0AA, telephone 020 7729 3000. In addition, many MPs, Assembly members, MSPs and MEPs hold regular local 'surgeries', where constituents can go in person to talk about issues that are of concern to them. These surgeries are often advertised in the local newspaper.

The government

The Prime Minister

The Prime Minister (PM) is the leader of the political party in power. He or she appoints the members of the cabinet (see below) and has control over many important public appointments. The official home of the Prime Minister is 10 Downing Street, in central London, near the Houses of Parliament. He or she also has a country house outside London called Chequers.

The Prime Minister can be changed if the MPs in the governing party decide to do so, or if he or she wishes to resign. The Prime Minister usually resigns if his or her party loses a General Election.

The cabinet

The Prime Minister appoints about 20 senior MPs to become ministers in charge of departments. These include:

- **Chancellor of the Exchequer** – responsible for the economy
- **Home Secretary** – responsible for crime, policing and immigration
- **Foreign Secretary** – responsible for managing relationships with foreign countries
- Other ministers (called 'Secretaries of State') responsible for subjects such as education, health and defence.

These ministers form the cabinet, a committee which usually meets weekly and makes important decisions about government policy. Many of these decisions have to be debated or approved by Parliament.

Each department also has a number of other ministers, called Ministers of State and Parliamentary Under-Secretaries of State, who take charge of particular areas of the department's work.

The opposition

The second-largest party in the House of Commons is called the opposition. The leader of the opposition usually becomes Prime Minister if his or her party wins the next General Election.

The leader of the opposition leads his or her party in pointing out what they see as the government's failures and weaknesses. One important opportunity to do this is at Prime Minister's Questions, which takes place every week while Parliament is sitting. The leader

The UK government, the law and your role - The government

of the opposition also appoints senior opposition MPs to be 'shadow ministers'. They form the shadow cabinet and their role is to challenge the government and put forward alternative policies.

The party system

Anyone aged 18 or over can stand for election as an MP but they are unlikely to win unless they have been nominated to represent one of the major political parties. These are the Conservative Party, the Labour Party, the Liberal Democrats, or one of the parties representing Scottish, Welsh or Northern Irish interests.

There are a few MPs who do not represent any of the main political parties. They are called 'independents' and usually represent an issue important to their constituency.

The main political parties actively look for members of the public to join their debates, contribute to their costs, and help at elections for Parliament or for local government. They have branches in most constituencies and hold policy-making conferences every year.

Pressure and lobby groups are organisations which try to influence government policy. They play an important role in politics. Some are representative organisations such as the CBI (Confederation of British Industry), which represents the views of British business. Others campaign on particular topics, such as the environment (for example, Greenpeace) or human rights (for example, Liberty).

The civil service

Civil servants support the government in developing and implementing its policies. They also deliver public services. Civil servants are accountable to ministers. They are chosen on merit and are politically neutral – they are not political appointees. People can apply to join the civil service through an application process, like other jobs in the UK. Civil servants are expected to carry out their role with dedication and a commitment to the civil service and its core values. These are: integrity, honesty, objectivity and impartiality (including being politically neutral).

Local government

Towns, cities and rural areas in the UK are governed by democratically elected councils, often called 'local authorities'. Some areas have both district and county councils, which have different functions. Most large towns and cities have a single local authority.

Local authorities provide a range of services in their areas. They are funded by money from central government and by local taxes.

Many local authorities appoint a mayor, who is the ceremonial leader of the council. In some towns, a mayor is elected to be the effective leader of the administration. London has 33 local authorities, with the Greater London Authority and the Mayor of London coordinating policies across the capital. For most local authorities, local elections for councillors are held in May every year. Many candidates stand for council election as members of a political party.

Devolved administrations

Since 1997, some powers have been devolved from the central government to give people in Wales, Scotland and Northern Ireland more control over matters that directly affect them. There has been a Welsh Assembly and a Scottish Parliament since 1999. There is also a Northern Ireland Assembly, although this has been suspended on a few occasions. Policy and laws governing defence, foreign affairs, immigration, taxation and social security all remain under central UK government control. However, many other public services, such as education, are controlled by the devolved administrations.
The devolved administrations each have their own civil service.

The Welsh government

The Welsh government and National Assembly for Wales are based in Cardiff, the capital city of Wales. The National Assembly has 60 Assembly members (AMs) and elections are held every four years using a form of proportional representation. Members can speak in either Welsh or English and all of the Assembly's publications are in both languages.
The Assembly has the power to make laws for Wales in 20 areas, including:

- education and training
- health and social services
- economic development
- housing

Since 2011, the National Assembly for Wales has been able to pass laws on these topics without the agreement of the UK Parliament.

The Scottish Parliament

The Scottish Parliament was formed in 1999. It sits in Edinburgh, the capital city of Scotland. There are 129 members of the Scottish Parliament (MSPs), elected by a form of proportional representation. The Scottish Parliament can pass laws for Scotland on all matters which are not specifically reserved to the UK Parliament. The matters on which the Scottish Parliament can legislate include:

- civil and criminal law
- health
- education
- planning
- additional tax-raising powers.

The Northern Ireland Assembly

A Northern Ireland Parliament was established in 1922, when Ireland was divided, but it was abolished in 1972, shortly after the Troubles broke out in 1969 (see The Partition of Ireland).

The Northern Ireland Assembly was established soon after the Belfast Agreement (or Good Friday Agreement) in 1998. There is a power-sharing agreement which distributes ministerial Offices amongst the main parties. The Assembly has 108 elected members, known as MLAs (members of the Legislative Assembly). They are elected with a form of proportional representation.

The Northern Ireland Assembly can make decisions on issues such as:

- education
- agriculture
- the environment
- health
- social services.

The UK government has the power to suspend all devolved assemblies. It has used this power several times in Northern Ireland when local political leaders found it difficult to work together. However, the Assembly has been running successfully since 2007.

Wales - 1999 - Cardiff
National Assembly - 60 members
- education and training
- health and social services
- economic development
- housing

Scotland - 1999 - Edinburgh
Scottish Parliament - 129 members
- civil and criminal law
- health
- education
- planning
- tax-raising powers

Northern Ireland - 1998 - Belfast
NI Assembly - 108 members
- education
- agriculture
- the environment
- health
- social services

The media and government
Proceedings in Parliament are broadcast on television and published in official reports called Hansard. Written reports can be found in large libraries and at www.parliament.uk. Most people get information about political issues and events from newspapers (often called 'the press'), television, radio and the internet.

The UK has a free press. This means that what is written in newspapers is free from government control. Some newspaper owners and editors hold strong political opinions and run campaigns to try to influence government policy and public opinion.

By law, radio and television coverage of the political parties must be balanced and so equal time has to be given to rival viewpoints.

Who can vote?

The UK has had a fully democratic voting system since 1928 (see The Development of British Democracy). The present voting age of 18 was set in 1969 and (with a few exceptions) all UK-born and naturalised adult citizens have the right to vote.

Adult citizens of the UK, and citizens of the Commonwealth and the Irish Republic who are resident in the UK, can vote in all public elections. Adult citizens of other EU states who are resident in the UK can vote in all elections except General Elections.

The electoral register
To be able to vote in a parliamentary, local or European election, you must have your name on the electoral register.

If you are eligible to vote, you can register by contacting your local council electoral registration Office. This is usually based at your local council (in Scotland it may be based elsewhere). If you don't know which local authority you come under, you can find out by visiting www.aboutmyvote.co.uk and entering your postcode. You can also download voter registration forms in English, Welsh and some other languages.

The electoral register is updated every year in September or October. An electoral registration form is sent to every household and this has to be completed and returned with the names of everyone who is resident in the household and eligible to vote.

In Northern Ireland a different system operates. This is called 'individual registration' and all those entitled to vote must complete their own registration form. Once registered, people stay on the register provided their personal details do not change. For more information see the Electoral Office for Northern Ireland website at www.eoni.org.uk

By law, each local authority has to make its electoral register available for anyone to look at, although this has to be supervised. The register is kept at each local electoral registration Office (or council Office in England and Wales). It is also possible to see the register at some public buildings such as libraries.

Where to vote

People vote in elections at places called polling stations, or polling places in Scotland. Before the election you will be sent a poll card. This tells you where your polling station or polling place is and when the election will take place. On election day, the polling station or place will be open from 7.00 am until 10.00 pm.

When you arrive at the polling station, the staff will ask for your name and address. In Northern Ireland you will also have to show photographic identification. You will then get your ballot paper, which you take to a polling booth to fill in privately. You should make up your own mind who to vote for. No one has the right to make you vote for a particular candidate. You should follow the instructions on the ballot paper. Once you have completed it, put it in the ballot box.

If it is difficult for you to get to a polling station or polling place, you can register for a postal ballot. Your ballot paper will be sent to your home before the election. You then fill it in and post it back. You can choose to do this when you register to vote.

Standing for office

Most citizens of the UK, the Irish Republic or the Commonwealth aged 18 or over can stand for public Office.

There are some exceptions, including:

- members of the armed forces
- civil servants
- people found guilty of certain criminal offences.

Members of the House of Lords may not stand for election to the House of Commons but are eligible for all other public Offices.

Visiting Parliament and the devolved administrations

The UK Parliament

The public can listen to debates in the Palace of Westminster from public galleries in both the House of Commons and the House of Lords.

You can write to your local MP in advance to ask for tickets or you can queue on the day at the public entrance. Entrance is free. Sometimes there are long queues for the House of Commons and people have to wait for at least one to two hours. It is usually easier to get in to the House of Lords.

You can find further information on the UK Parliament website at www.parliament.uk.

Northern Ireland Assembly

In Northern Ireland elected members, known as MLAs, meet in the Northern Ireland Assembly at Stormont, in Belfast.

The UK government, the law and your role - Who can vote

There are two ways to arrange a visit to Stormont. You can either contact the Education Service (details are on the Northern Ireland Assembly website at www.niassembly.gov.uk) or contact an MLA.

Scottish Parliament
In Scotland the elected members, called MSPs, meet in the Scottish Parliament building at Holyrood in Edinburgh (for more information, see www.scottish.parliament.uk).

You can get information, book tickets or arrange tours through visitor services. You can write to them at the Scottish Parliament, Edinburgh, EH99 1SP, telephone 0131 348 5200 or email sp.bookings@scottish.parliament.uk

National Assembly for Wales
In Wales the elected members, known as AMs, meet in the Welsh Assembly in the Senedd in Cardiff Bay (for more information, see www.wales.gov.uk).

The Senedd is an open building. You can book guided tours or seats in the public galleries for the Welsh Assembly. To make a booking, contact the Assembly Booking Service on 0845 010 5500 or email assembly.bookings@wales.gsi.gov.uk.

Welsh National Assembly
60 AM (Assembly Members)
Located in the Senedd Cardfiff Bay

Scottish Parliament
129 MSP (Members of the Scottish Parliament)
Located in Holyrood in Edinburgh

Northern Ireland Assembly
108 MLA (Members of the Legislative Assembly)
Located at Stormont, in Belfast.

The UK government, the law and your role - The UK and international institutions

The UK and international institutions

The Commonwealth

The Commonwealth is an association of countries that support each other and work together towards shared goals in democracy and development. Most member states were once part of the British Empire, although a few countries which were not have also joined. The Queen is the ceremonial head of the Commonwealth, which currently has 54 member states (see below). Membership is voluntary. The Commonwealth has no power over its members, although it can suspend membership. The Commonwealth is based on the core values of democracy, good government and the rule of law.

Commonwealth members:

Antigua and Barbuda	Kenya	Singapore
Australia	Kiribati	Solomon Islands
The Bahamas	Lesotho	South Africa
Bangladesh	Malawi	Sri Lanka
Barbados	Malaysia	St Kitts and Nevis
Belize	Maldives	St Lucia
Botswana	Malta	St Vincent and the Grenadines
Brunei Darussalam	Mauritius	
Cameroon	Mozambique	Swaziland
Canada	Namibia	Tanzania
Cyprus	Nauru	Tonga
Dominica	New Zealand	Trinidad and Tobago
Fiji (currently suspended)	Nigeria	Tuvalu
The Gambia	Pakistan	Uganda
Ghana	Papua New Guinea	UK
Grenada	Rwanda	Vanuatu
Guyana	Samoa	Zambia
India	Seychelles	
Jamaica	Sierra Leone	

The European Union

The European Union (EU), originally called the European Economic Community (EEC), was set up by six western European countries (Belgium, France, Germany, Italy, Luxembourg and the Netherlands) who signed the Treaty of Rome on 25 March 1957. The UK originally decided not to join this group but it became a member in 1973. There are now 28 EU member states (see below). However, following the "Brexit" referendum on 23 June 2016, the UK voted to leave the EU and it is anticipated that the process will be initiated in 2017 to last approximately 2 years.

EU member states (as of May 2019)

Austria	Estonia	Italy	Portugal
Belgium	Finland	Latvia	Romania
Bulgaria	France	Lithuania	Slovakia
Croatia	Germany	Luxembourg	Slovenia
Cyprus	Greece	Malta	Spain
Czech Republic	Hungary	Netherlands	Sweden
Denmark	Ireland	Poland	UK

EU law is legally binding in the UK and all the other EU member states. European laws are called directives, regulations or framework decisions.

The Council of Europe
The Council of Europe is separate from the EU. It has 47 member countries, including the UK, and is responsible for the protection and promotion of human rights in those countries. It has no power to make laws but draws up conventions and charters, the most well-known of which is the European Convention on Human Rights and Fundamental Freedoms, usually called the European Convention on Human Rights.

The United Nations
The UK is part of the United Nations (UN), an international organisation with more than 190 countries as members. The UN was set up after the Second World War and aims to prevent war and promote international peace and security. There are 15 members on the UN Security Council, which recommends action when there are international crises and threats to peace. The UK is one of five permanent members of the Security Council.

The North Atlantic Treaty Organization (NATO)
The UK is also a member of NATO. NATO is a group of European and North American countries that have agreed to help each other if they come under attack. It also aims to maintain peace between all of its members.

Respecting the law

One of the most important responsibilities of all residents in the UK is to know and obey the law. This section will tell you about the legal system in the UK and some of the laws that may affect you. Britain is proud of being a welcoming country, but all residents, regardless of their background, are expected to comply with the law and to understand that some things which may be allowed in other legal systems are not acceptable in the UK.

Those who do not respect the law should not expect to be allowed to become permanent residents in the UK.

The law is relevant to all areas of life in the UK. You should make sure that you are aware of the laws which affect your everyday life, including both your personal and business affairs.

The law in the UK

Every person in the UK receives equal treatment under the law. This means that the law applies in the same way to everyone, no matter who they are or where they are from. Laws can be divided into criminal law and civil law:

- Criminal law relates to crimes, which are usually investigated by the police or another authority such as a council, and which are punished by the courts.
- Civil law is used to settle disputes between individuals or groups.

Examples of criminal laws

- Carrying a weapon: it is a criminal offence to carry a weapon of any kind, even if it is for self-defence. This includes a gun, a knife or anything that is made or adapted to cause injury.
- Drugs: selling or buying drugs such as heroin, cocaine, ecstasy and cannabis is illegal in the UK.
- Racial crime: it is a criminal offence to cause harassment, alarm or distress to someone because of their religion or ethnic origin.
- Selling tobacco: it is illegal to sell tobacco products (for example, cigarettes, cigars, roll-up tobacco) to anyone under the age of 18.
- Smoking in public places: it is against the law to smoke tobacco products in nearly every enclosed public place in the UK. There are signs displayed to tell you where you cannot smoke.
- Buying alcohol: it is a criminal offence to sell alcohol to anyone who is under 18 or to buy alcohol for people who are under the age of 18. (There is one exception: people aged 16 or over can drink alcohol with a meal in a hotel or restaurant – see Pubs and Night Clubs.)
- Drinking in public: some places have alcohol-free zones where you cannot drink in public. The police can also confiscate alcohol or move young people on from public places. You can be fined or arrested.

This list does not include all crimes. There are many that apply in most countries, such as murder, theft and assault. You can find out more about types of crime in the UK at www.gov.uk.

The UK government, the law and your role - Respecting the law

Examples of civil laws

- Housing law: this includes disputes between landlords and tenants over issues such as repairs and eviction.
- Consumer rights: an example of this is a dispute about faulty goods or services.
- Employment law: these cases include disputes over wages and cases of unfair dismissal or discrimination in the workplace.
- Debt: people might be taken to court if they owe money to someone.
- The police and their duties

The job of the police in the UK is to:
- protect life and property
- prevent disturbances (also known as keeping the peace)
- prevent and detect crime.

The police are organised into a number of separate police forces headed by Chief Constables. They are independent of the government.

In November 2012, the public elected Police and Crime Commissioners (PCCs) in England and Wales. These are directly elected individuals who are responsible for the delivery of an efficient and effective police force that reflects the needs of their local communities. PCCs set local police priorities and the local policing budget. They also appoint the Chief Constable.

The police force is a public service that helps and protects everyone, no matter what their background or where they live. Police Officers must themselves obey the law. They must not misuse their authority, make a false statement, be rude or abusive, or commit racial discrimination. If police Officers are corrupt or misuse their authority they are severely punished.

Police Officers are supported by police community support Officers (PSCOs). PSCOs have different roles according to the area but usually patrol the streets, work with the public, and support police Officers at crime scenes and major events.

All people in the UK are expected to help the police prevent and detect crimes whenever they can. If you are arrested and taken to a police station, a police Officer will tell you the reason for your arrest and you will be able to seek legal advice.

If something goes wrong, the police complaints system tries to put it right. Anyone can make a complaint about the police by going to a police station or writing to the Chief Constable of the police force involved. Complaints can also be made to an independent body: the Independent Police Complaints Commission in England and Wales, the Police Complaints Commissioner for Scotland or the Police Ombudsman for Northern Ireland.

Terrorism and extremism

The UK faces a range of terrorist threats. The most serious of these is from Al Qa'ida, its affiliates and like-minded organisations. The UK also faces threats from other kinds of terrorism, such as Northern Ireland-related terrorism.

All terrorist groups try to radicalise and recruit people to their cause. How, where and to what extent they try to do so will vary. Evidence shows that these groups attract very low levels of public support, but people who want to make their home in the UK should be aware of this threat. It is important that all citizens feel safe. This includes feeling safe from all kinds of extremism (vocal or active opposition to fundamental British values), including religious extremism and far-right extremism.

If you think someone is trying to persuade you to join an extremist or terrorist cause, you should notify your local police force.

Check that you understand:
- The difference between civil and criminal law and some examples of each
- The duties of the police
- The possible terrorist threats facing the UK

The role of the courts

The judiciary

Judges (who are together called 'the judiciary') are responsible for interpreting the law and ensuring that trials are conducted fairly. The government cannot interfere with this.

Sometimes the actions of the government are claimed to be illegal. If the judges agree, then the government must either change its policies or ask Parliament to change the law. If judges find that a public body is not respecting someone's legal rights, they can order that body to change its practices and/or pay compensation. Judges also make decisions in disputes between members of the public or organisations. These might be about contracts, property or employment rights or after an accident.

Criminal courts

There are some differences between the court systems in England and Wales, Scotland and Northern Ireland.

Magistrates' and Justice of the Peace Courts

In England, Wales and Northern Ireland, most minor criminal cases are dealt with in a Magistrates' Court. In Scotland, minor criminal offences go to a Justice of the Peace Court. Magistrates and Justices of the Peace (JPs) are members of the local community. In England, Wales and Scotland they usually work unpaid and do not need legal qualifications. They receive training to do the job and are supported by a legal adviser. Magistrates decide the verdict in each case that comes before them and, if the person is found guilty, the sentence that they are given. In Northern Ireland, cases are heard by a District Judge or Deputy District Judge, who is legally qualified and paid.

Crown Courts and Sheriff Courts

In England, Wales and Northern Ireland, serious offences are tried in front of a judge and a jury in a Crown Court. In Scotland, serious cases are heard in a Sheriff Court with either a sheriff or a sheriff with a jury. The most serious cases in Scotland, such as murder, are heard at a High Court with a judge and jury. A jury is made up of members of the public chosen at random from the local electoral register (see The Electoral Register). In England, Wales and Northern Ireland a jury has 12 members, and in Scotland a jury has 15 members. Everyone who is summoned to do jury service must do it unless they are not eligible (for example, because they have a criminal conviction) or they provide a good reason to be excused, such as ill health.

The jury has to listen to the evidence presented at the trial and then decide a verdict of 'guilty' or 'not guilty' based on what they have heard. In Scotland, a third verdict of 'not proven' is also possible. If the jury finds a defendant guilty, the judge decides on the penalty.

Youth Courts

In England, Wales and Northern Ireland, if an accused person is aged 10 to 17, the case is normally heard in a Youth Court in front of up to three specially trained magistrates or a District Judge. The most serious cases will go to the Crown Court. The parents or carers of the young person are expected to attend the hearing. Members of the public are not allowed in Youth Courts, and the name or photographs of the accused young person cannot be published in newspapers or used by the media.

In Scotland a system called the Children's Hearings System is used to deal with children and young people who have committed an offence.

Northern Ireland has a system of youth conferencing to consider how a child should be dealt with when they have committed an offence.

Civil courts

County Courts

County Courts deal with a wide range of civil disputes. These include people trying to get back money that is owed to them, cases involving personal injury, family matters, breaches of contract, and divorce. In Scotland, most of these matters are dealt with in the Sheriff Court. More serious civil cases – for example, when a large amount of compensation is being claimed – are dealt with in the High Court in England, Wales and Northern Ireland. In Scotland, they are dealt with in the Court of Session in Edinburgh.

The small claims procedure

The small claims procedure is an informal way of helping people to settle minor disputes without spending a lot of time and money using a lawyer. This procedure is used for claims of less than £10,000 in England and Wales and £5,000 in Scotland and Northern Ireland. The hearing is held in front of a judge in an ordinary room, and people from both sides of the dispute sit around a table. Small claims can also be issued online through Money Claims Online (www.moneyclaim.gov.uk).

You can get details about the small claims procedure from your local County Court or Sheriff Court. Details of your local court can be found as follows:

- England and Wales: at www.gov.uk
- Scotland: at www.scotcourts.gov.uk
- Northern Ireland: at www.courtsni.gov.uk.

Small claims
England and Wales:
£10.000
N. Ireland and Scotland:
£5.000

Legal advice

Solicitors

Solicitors are trained lawyers who give advice on legal matters, take action for their clients and represent their clients in court.

There are solicitors' Offices throughout the UK. It is important to find out which aspects of law a solicitor specialises in and to check that they have the right experience to help you with your case. Many advertise in local newspapers and in Yellow Pages. The Citizens Advice Bureau (www.citizensadvice.org.uk) can give you names of local solicitors and which areas of law they specialise in. You can also get this information from the Law Society (www.lawsociety.org.uk) in England and Wales, the Law Society of Scotland (www.lawscot.org.uk) or the Law Society of Northern Ireland (www.lawsoc-ni.org). Solicitors' charges are usually based on how much time they spend on a case. It is very important to find out at the start how much a case is likely to cost.

Fundamental principles

Britain has a long history of respecting an individual's rights and ensuring essential freedoms. These rights have their roots in Magna Carta, the Habeas Corpus Act and the Bill of Rights of 1689 (see Legal and Political Changes, The Restoration and Constitutional Monarcy – A Bill of Rights), and they have developed over a period of time. British diplomats and lawyers had an important role in drafting the European Convention on Human Rights and Fundamental Freedoms. The UK was one of the first countries to sign the Convention in 1950.
Some of the principles included in the European Convention on Human Rights are:

- right to life
- prohibition of torture
- prohibition of slavery and forced labour
- right to liberty and security
- right to a fair trial
- freedom of thought, conscience and religion
- freedom of expression (speech).

The Human Rights Act 1998 incorporated the European Convention on Human Rights into UK law. The government, public bodies and the courts must follow the principles of the Convention.

Equal opportunities
UK laws ensure that people are not treated unfairly in any area of life or work because of their age, disability, sex, pregnancy and maternity, race, religion or belief, sexuality or marital status. If you face problems with discrimination, you can get more information from the Citizens Advice Bureau or from one of the following organisations:

- England and Wales: Equality and Human Rights Commission (www.equalityhumanrights.com)
- Scotland: Equality and Human Rights Commission in Scotland (www.equalityhumanrights.com/scotland/the-commission-inscotland) and Scottish Human Rights Commission (www.scottishhumanrights.com)
- Northern Ireland: Equality Commission for Northern Ireland (www.equalityni.org)
- Northern Ireland Human Rights Commission (www.nihrc.org).

Domestic violence
In the UK, brutality and violence in the home is a serious crime. Anyone who is violent towards their partner – whether they are a man or woman, married or living together

– can be prosecuted. Any man who forces a woman to have sex, including a woman's husband, can be charged with rape.

It is important for anyone facing domestic violence to get help as soon as possible. A solicitor or the Citizens Advice Bureau can explain the available options. In some areas there are safe places to go and stay in, called refuges or shelters. There are emergency telephone numbers in the helpline section at the front of Yellow Pages, including, for women, the number of the nearest women's centre. You can also phone the 24-hour National Domestic Violence Freephone Helpline on 0808 2000 247 at any time, or the police can help you find a safe place to stay.

Female genital mutilation
Female genital mutilation (FGM), also known as cutting or female circumcision, is illegal in the UK. Practising FGM or taking a girl or woman abroad for FGM is a criminal offence.

Forced marriage
A marriage should be entered into with the full and free consent of both people involved. Arranged marriages, where both parties agree to the marriage, are acceptable in the UK. Forced marriage is where one or both parties do not or cannot give their consent to enter into the partnership. Forcing another person to marry is a criminal offence.

Forced Marriage Protection Orders were introduced in 2008 for England, Wales and Northern Ireland under the Forced Marriage (Civil Protection) Act 2007. Court orders can be obtained to protect a person from being forced into a marriage, or to protect a person in a forced marriage. Similar Protection Orders were introduced in Scotland in November 2011.

A potential victim, or someone acting for them, can apply for an order. Anyone found to have breached an order can be jailed for up to two years for contempt of court.

Taxation

Income tax
People in the UK have to pay tax on their income, which includes:

- wages from paid employment
- profits from self-employment
- taxable benefits
- pensions
- income from property, savings and dividends.

Money raised from income tax pays for government services such as roads, education, police and the armed forces.

For most people, the right amount of income tax is automatically taken from their income from employment by their employer and paid directly to HM Revenue & Customs (HMRC), the government department that collects taxes. This system is called 'Pay As You Earn' (PAYE). If you are self-employed, you need to pay your own tax through a system called 'self-assessment', which includes completing a tax return. Other people may also need to complete a tax return. If HMRC sends you a tax return, it is important to complete and return the form as soon as you have all the necessary information.

You can find out more about income tax at www.hmrc.gov.uk/incometax. You can get help and advice about taxes and completing tax forms from the HMRC self-assessment helpline, on 0845 300 0627, and the HMRC website at www.hmrc.gov.uk.

National insurance
Almost everybody in the UK who is in paid work, including self-employed people, must pay National Insurance Contributions. The money raised from National Insurance Contributions is used to pay for state benefits and services such as the state retirement pension and the National Health Service (NHS).

Employees have their National Insurance Contributions deducted from their pay by their employer. People who are self-employed need to pay National Insurance Contributions themselves. Anyone who does not pay enough National Insurance Contributions will not be able to receive certain contributory benefits such as Jobseeker's Allowance or a full state retirement pension. Some workers, such as part-time workers, may not qualify for statutory payments such as maternity pay if they do not earn enough.

Further guidance about National Insurance Contributions is available on HMRC's website at www.hmrc.gov.uk/ni.

Getting a National Insurance number
A National Insurance number is a unique personal account number. It makes sure that the National Insurance Contributions and tax you pay are properly recorded against your name. All young people in the UK are sent a National Insurance number just before their 16th birthday.

A non-UK national living in the UK and looking for work, starting work or setting up as self-employed will need a National Insurance number. However, you can start work without one. If you have permission to work in the UK, you will need to telephone the Department for Work and Pensions (DWP) to arrange to get a National Insurance number. You may be required to attend an interview. The DWP will advise you of the appropriate application process and tell you which documents you will need to bring to an interview if one is necessary. You will usually need documents that prove your identity and that you have permission to work in the UK. A National Insurance number does not on its own prove to an employer that you have the right to work in the UK.

You can find out more information about how to apply for a National Insurance number at www.gov.uk.

Driving

In the UK, you must be at least 17 years old to drive a car or motor cycle and you must have a driving licence to drive on public roads. To get a UK driving licence you must pass a driving test, which tests both your knowledge and your practical skills. You need to be at least 16 years old to ride a moped, and there are other age requirements and special tests for driving large vehicles.

Drivers can use their driving licence until they are 70 years old. After that, the licence is valid for three years at a time.

In Northern Ireland, a newly qualified driver must display an 'R' place (for restricted driver) for one year after passing the test.

If your driving licence is from a country in the European Union (EU), Iceland, Liechtenstein or Norway, you can drive in the UK for as long as your licence is valid. If you have a licence from any other country, you may use it in the UK for up to 12 months. To continue driving after that, you must get a UK full driving licence. Be mindful however that as the UK leaves the EU from 2017, such legislation may change.

If you are resident in the UK, your car or motor cycle must be registered at the Driver and Vehicle Licensing Agency (DVLA). You must pay an annual road tax and display the tax disc, which shows that the tax has been paid, on the windscreen. You must also have valid motor insurance. It is a serious criminal offence to drive without insurance. If your vehicle is over three years old, you must take it for a Ministry of Transport (MOT) test every year. It is an offence not to have an MOT certificate if your vehicle is more than three years old. You can find out more about vehicle tax and MOT requirements from www.gov.uk.

Your role in the community

Becoming a British citizen or settling in the UK brings responsibilities but also opportunities. Everyone has the opportunity to participate in their community. This section looks at some of the responsibilities of being a citizen and gives information about how you can help to make your community a better place to live and work.

Values and responsibilities

Although Britain is one of the world's most diverse societies, there is a set of shared values and responsibilities that everyone can agree with.
These values and responsibilities include:

- to obey and respect the law
- to be aware of the rights of others and respect those rights
- to treat others with fairness

- to behave responsibly
- to help and protect your family
- to respect and preserve the environment
- to treat everyone equally, regardless of sex, race, religion, age, disability, class or sexual orientation
- to work to provide for yourself and your family
- to help others
- to vote in local and national government elections.

Taking on these values and responsibilities will make it easier for you to become a full and active citizen.

Being a good neighbour
When you move into a new house or apartment, introduce yourself to the people who live near you. Getting to know your neighbours can help you to become part of the community and make friends. Your neighbours are also a good source of help – for example, they may be willing to feed your pets if you are away, or offer advice on local shops and services.

You can help prevent any problems and conflicts with your neighbours by respecting their privacy and limiting how much noise you make. Also try to keep your garden tidy, and only put your refuse bags and bins on the street or in communal areas if they are due to be collected.

Getting involved in local activities
Volunteering and helping your community are an important part of being a good citizen. They enable you to integrate and get to know other people. It helps to make your community a better place if residents support each other. It also helps you to fulfil your duties as a citizen, such as behaving responsibly and helping others.

How you can support your community

There are a number of positive ways in which you can support your community and be a good citizen.

Jury service
As well as getting the right to vote, people on the electoral register are randomly selected to serve on a jury. Anyone who is on the electoral register and is aged 18 to 70 can be asked to do this.

The UK government, the law and your role - How you can support your community

Helping in schools

If you have children, there are many ways in which you can help at their schools. Parents can often help in classrooms, by supporting activities or listening to children read.

Many schools organise events to raise money for extra equipment or out-of-school activities. Activities might include book sales, toy sales or bringing food to sell. You might have good ideas of your own for raising money. Sometimes events are organised by parent-teacher associations (PTAs). Volunteering to help with their events or joining the association is a way of doing something good for the school and also making new friends in your local community. You can find out about these opportunities from notices in the school or notes your children bring home.

School governors and school boards

School governors, or members of the school board in Scotland, are people from the local community who wish to make a positive contribution to children's education. They must be aged 18 or over at the date of their election or appointment. There is no upper age limit.

Governors and school boards have an important part to play in raising school standards. They have three key roles:

- setting the strategic direction of the school
- ensuring accountability
- monitoring and evaluating school performance.
- You can contact your local school to ask if they need a new governor or school board member. In England, you can also apply online at the School Governors' One-Stop Shop at www.sgoss.org.uk. In England, parents and other community groups can apply to open a free school in their local area. More information about this can be found on the Department for Education website at www.dfe.gov.uk.

Supporting political parties

Political parties welcome new members. Joining one is a way to demonstrate your support for certain views and to get involved in the democratic process.

Political parties are particularly busy at election times. Members work hard to persuade people to vote for their candidates – for instance, by handing out leaflets in the street or by knocking on people's doors and asking for their support. This is called 'canvassing'. You don't have to tell a canvasser how you intend to vote if you don't want to.

British citizens can stand for Office as a local councillor, a member of Parliament (or the devolved equivalents) or a member of the European Parliament. This is an opportunity to become even more involved in the political life of the UK. You may also be able to stand for Office if you are an Irish citizen, an eligible Commonwealth citizen or (except for standing to be an MP) a citizen of another EU country.

You can find out more about joining a political party from the individual party websites.

Helping with local services

There are opportunities to volunteer with a wide range of local service providers, including local hospitals and youth projects. Services often want to involve local people in decisions about the way in which they work. Universities, housing associations, museums and arts councils may advertise for people to serve as volunteers in their governing bodies.

You can volunteer with the police, and become a special constable or a lay (non-police) representative. You can also apply to become a magistrate. You will often find advertisements for vacancies in your local newspaper or on local radio. You can also find out more about these sorts of roles at www.gov.uk.

Blood and organ donation

Donated blood is used by hospitals to help people with a wide range of injuries and illnesses. Giving blood only takes about an hour to do. You can register to give blood at:

- England and North Wales: www.blood.co.uk
- Rest of Wales: www.welsh-blood.org.uk
- Scotland: www.scotblood.co.uk
- Northern Ireland: www.nibts.org

Many people in the UK are waiting for organ transplants. If you register to be an organ donor, it can make it easier for your family to decide whether to donate your organs when you die. You can register to be an organ donor at www.organdonation.nhs.uk. Living people can also donate a kidney.

Other ways to volunteer

Volunteering is working for good causes without payment. There are many benefits to volunteering, such as meeting new people helping make your community a better place. Some volunteer activities will give you a chance to practise your English or develop work skills that will help you find a job or improve your curriculum vitae (CV). Many people volunteer simply because they want to help other people.

Activities you can do as a volunteer include:

- working with animals – for example, caring for animals at a local rescue shelter
- youth work – for example, volunteering at a youth group
- helping improve the environment – for example, participating in a litter pick-up in the local area
- working with the homeless in, for example, a homelessness shelter
- mentoring – for example, supporting someone who has just come out of prison
- work in health and hospitals – for example, working on an information desk in a hospital
- helping older people at, for example, a residential care home.

There are thousands of active charities and voluntary organisations in the UK. They work to improve the lives of people, animals and the environment in many different ways. They range from the British branches of international organisations, such as the British Red Cross, to small local charities working in particular areas. They include charities working with older people (such as Age UK), with children (for example, the National Society for the Prevention of Cruelty to Children (NSPCC)), and with the homeless (for example, Crisis and Shelter). There are also medical research charities (for example, Cancer Research UK), environmental charities (including the National Trust and Friends of the Earth) and charities working with animals (such as the People's Dispensary for Sick Animals (PDSA)).

Volunteers are needed to help with their activities and to raise money. The charities often advertise in local newspapers, and most have websites that include information about their opportunities. You can also get information about volunteering for different organisations from www.do-it.org.uk.

There are many opportunities for young people to volunteer and receive accreditation which will help them to develop their skills. These include the National Citizen Service programme, which gives 16- and 17-year-olds the opportunity to enjoy outdoor activities, develop their skills and take part in a community project. You can find out more about these opportunities as follows:

- National Citizen Service: at nationalcitizenservice.direct.gov.uk
- England: at www.vinspired.com
- Wales: at www.gwirvol.org
- Scotland: at www.vds.org.uk
- Northern Ireland: at www.volunteernow.co.uk

Looking after the environment

It is important to recycle as much of your waste as you can. Using recycled materials to make new products uses less energy and means that we do not need to extract more raw materials from the earth. It also means that less rubbish is created, so the amount being put into landfill is reduced.

You can learn more about recycling and its benefits at www.recyclenow.com. At this website you can also find out what you can recycle at home and in the local area if you live in England. This information is available:

- for Wales at www.wasteawarenesswales.org.uk
- for Scotland at www.recycleforscotland.com
- and for Northern Ireland from your local authority.

A good way to support your local community is to shop for products locally where you can. This will help businesses and farmers in your area and in Britain. It will also reduce your carbon footprint, because the products you buy will not have had to travel as far.

Walking and using public transport to get around when you can is also a good way to protect the environment. It means that you create less pollution than when you use a car.

The UK government, the law and your role

Test your knowledge

1. Members of the European Parliament (MEPs) are elected on the basis of:
A. Personal achievements
B. Instant run-off
C. First past the post system (the candidate who gets the most votes)
D. Proportional representation

2. The House of Commons is normally more independent of the government than the House of Lords:
A. True
B. False

3. Who is the ceremonial head of the Commonwealth?
A. The British Queen
B. The Pope
C. The President of the United States
D. The Prime Minister of the UK

4. On which of the following issues the Northern Ireland Assembly CANNOT make decisions?
A. Health
B. Education
C. The Environment
D. Planning

5. What was celebrated at the Diamond Jubilee in 2012?
A. 60 years of Elizabeth II as Queen
B. 50 years of Elizabeth II as Queen
C. The Olympic Games taking place in the UK
D. The success of the British poetry

6. Who is responsible for managing relationships with foreign countries?
A. The Chancellor of the Exchequer
B. The Foreign Secretary
C. The Home Secretary
D. The Queen

The UK government, the law and your role

7. Which of the following is NOT a devolved administration?
A. The Scottish Parliament
B. The Welsh Assembly
C. The Irish Parliament
D. The Northern Ireland Assembly

8. Which TWO of the following charities work with homeless people?
A. Friends of the Earth
B. Shelter
C. Crisis
D. Oxfam

9. Which of the following is a criminal offence?
A. Selling tobacco to someone under the age of 18
B. Owing money to someone
C. Discrimination in the workplace
D. Selling faulty goods or services

10. Which Court deals with the most serious civil cases in England, Wales and Northern Ireland?
A. The County Court
B. The Crown Court
C. The High Court
D. The Sheriff Court

Answers: 1.D - 2.B - 3.A - 4.D - 5.A - 6.B - 7.C - 8.B,C - 9.A - 10.C

REVISION

REVISION NOTES

Monarchs

This is the chronological order of all monarchs in the UK. The third column provides some information about their connection to the previous monarch.
You do not need to know all the dates and monarchs for the test, this is for information.

English Kings

Dates	Name	Relationship to previous
827 - 839	EGBERT	First monarch
839-856	AETHELWULF	Son
856 - 860	AETHELBALD	Son
860 - 866	AETHELBERT	Brother
866 - 871	AETHELRED I	Brother
871 - 899	ALFRED THE GREAT	Son
924 - 939	ATHELSTAN	Son
939 - 946	EDMUND	Half brother
946 - 955	EADRED	Son of Edward the Elder
955 - 959	EADWIG	Son of Edmund I
959 - 975	EDGAR	Son of Edmund I
975 - 978	EDWARD THE MARTYR	Son
978 - 1016	AETHELRED II THE UNREADY	Son of Edgar
1016 - 1016	EDMUND II IRONSIDE	Son
1016 - 1035	Canute the Dane aka Cnut the great	New line
1035 - 1040	HAROLD I	Illegitimate son of Canute
1040 - 1042	HARTHACANUTE	Son of Canute
1042-1066	EDWARD THE CONFESSOR	Half brother
1066	HAROLD II	Not related

Norman Kings

Dates	Name	Relationship to previous
1066- 1087	WILLIAM I	The Conqueror - Duke of Normandy, invaded England
1087- 1100	WILLIAM II	Son
1100-1135	HENRY I	Son of William I
1135-1154	Stephen	Grandson of William I

Plantagenet Kings

Dates	Name	Relationship to previous
1154-1189	HENRY II	New line
1189 - 1199	RICHARD I	Son of Henry II - Lionheart
1199 -1216	John	Son of Henry II
1216 -1272	HENRY III	Son

Monarchs of England and Wales

Dates	Name	Relationship to previous
1272 - 1307	EDWARD I	Son of Henry III
1307 - 1327	EDWARD II	Son - *deposed*
1327 - 1377	EDWARD III	Son
1377 - 1399	RICHARD II	Grandson of Edward III - *deposed*

House of Lancaster

Dates	Name	Relationship to previous
1399 - 1413	HENRY IV	Grandson of Edward III
1413 - 1422	HENRY V	Son
1422 - 1461	HENRY VI	Son

House of York

Dates	Name	Relationship to previous
1461- 1483	EDWARD IV	Grandson of Henry VI
1483 - 1483	EDWARD V	Son
1483 - 1485	RICHARD III	Brother of Edward IV

The Tudors

Dates	Name	Relationship to previous
1485 - 1509	HENRY VII	New dynasty
1509 - 1547	HENRY VIII	Son
1547 - 1553	EDWARD VI	Son
1553 - 1558	MARY I	Daughter of Henry VIII (Bloody Mary)
1558-1603	ELIZABETH I	Daughter of Henry VIII

The Stuarts

Dates	Name	Relationship to previous
1603 -1625	JAMES I and VI of Scotland	Son of Mary Queen of Scots
1625 - 1649	CHARLES 1	Son

The Commonwealth

Dates	Name	Relationship to previous
1653 - 1658	OLIVER CROMWELL	Lord Protector not King
1658 - 1659	RICHARD CROMWELL	Son - Lord Protector not King

The Restoration

The Restoration

Dates	Name	Relationship to previous
1660 - 1685	CHARLES II	Son of Charles I
1685 - 1688	JAMES II and VII of Scotland	Son of Charles I and brother to Charles II
1689 - 1702	WILLIAM III and Mary II	Grandson of Charles I
1702 - 1714	ANNE	Daughter of James II

The Hanovarians

Dates	Name	Relationship to previous
1714 -1727	GEORGE I	Great Grandson of James I
1727 - 1760	GEORGE II	Son
1760 - 1820	GEORGE III	Grandson of George II
1820 - 1830	GEORGE IV	Son
1830 - 1837	WILLIAM IV	Brother
1837 - 1901	VICTORIA	Grand-daughter of George III
1901 - 1910	EDWARD VII	Son

House of Windsor

Dates	Name	Relationship to previous
1910 - 1936	GEORGE V	Brother
1936	EDWARD VIII	Son - Abdicated
1936 - 1952	GEORGE VI	Brother
1952-	ELIZABETH II	daughter

Key Dates

This is a list in chronological order of the key dates in the official book. You don't need to know all of them for the test but you should have a good overall knowledge of the main period and when key events took place.

Year	Event
8000 BC	Channel forms
4000 BC	First farmers arrive in Britain
2000 BC	Bronze Age
55 BC	Julius Caesar and the Romans fail to invade Britain
43 AD	The romans successfully invade Britain
122 AD	Hadrian's wall construction begins
410 AD	The Roman army leaves
600	Anglo-Saxon kingdoms are established
789	The Vikings first come to Britain
1066	Battle of Hastings William of Normandy invade Britain
1215	Magna Carta makes the King subject to the Law
1284	King Edward I annexes Wales to England (Statute of Rhuddlan)
1314	Robert the Bruce leads the Scottish to victory against the English at the battle of Bannockburn
1348	The Black Death kills a third of population
1415	Battle of Agincourt: victory against the French and end of the Hundred Year War.
1455	Wars of the Roses begin between Houses of York and Lancaster
1485	Battle of Bosworth: King Richard III is killed by Henry Tudor of Lancaster. End of the Wars of Roses. Henry Tudor becomes King Henry VII
1560	Scottish Parliament abolishes the authority of the Pope and makes Roman Catholic service illegal
1588	Victory over the Spanish Armada
1603	Death of Elizabeth I. Her cousin, King James I succeeds her.
1641	Start of a rebellion in Ireland

Revision notes - Key Dates

1642	Civil war between King Charles I and the Parliament.
1646	Parliament wins and holds Charles I prisoner
1649	Charles I is executed
1656	Jews settle in London
1658	Death of Oliver Cromwell
1660	Parliament asks Charles II to come back from Exile
1665	Major outbreak of Plague in London
1666	Big fire of London
1679	Habeas Corpus. No one can be held prisoner unlawfully.
1685	Charles II's death. His brother becomes King James II of England and King James VII of Scotland
1688	Protestants ask William of Orange to invade England. There is little resistance. (Glorious Revolution).
1689	The Bill of Rights confirms the rights of Parliament and limits the King's power. Monarch must be Protestant and Parliament is elected every 3 years
1690	William defeats James II at the battle of the Boyne in Ireland.
1680-1720	Huguenots immigration. They are refugees from France.
1707	The Act of Union creates the Kingdom of Great Britain
1714	Queen Anne dies and George I becomes King
1721-1742	First Prime Minister in exercise: Sir Robert Walpole
1745	Charles Edward Stuart attempts to take the throne to restore the Stuart dynasty
1746	Battle of Culloden: George II wins against Charles Stuart. Scottish clans lose their power
Late 1700s	Quakers group oppose slavery
1776	13 colonies in America declare their independence
1783	Britain recognises the American colonies independence
1789	Revolution in France. France declares war on Britain
1801	The Act of Union creates the United Kingdom of Great Britain and Ireland. The Union Flag is created (called Union Jack)

Revision notes - Key Dates

1805	Victory against France at Trafalgar. Admiral Nelson is killed during the battle
1807	It becomes illegal to trade slaves on British ships
1815	End of the French Wars with the victory at Waterloo. Napoleon defeated by the Duke of Wellington (the Iron Duke)
1832	The Reform Act increases the number of people allowed to vote
1833	The Emancipation Act abolishes slavery. 2 million Chinese and Indians are employed to replace slaves
1837	Victoria becomes Queen
1846	Repealing of the Corn Laws opens up import
1847	Women and children working hours are limited to 10 hours per day
1853-1856	Crimean War against Russia
1867	Second Reform Act creates urban seats in Parliament and reduces the wealth needed to be allowed to vote
1870	Act of Parliament for married women allows them to keep their earnings
1882	Second act of Parliament for married women allows them to own their own property
1899-1902	The Boer War in South Africa against settlers from Netherland called Boers.
1913	Home Rule Bill for Ireland proposes Ireland to have its own parliament. It is opposed by protestants from North Ireland
1914	The Archduke Franz Ferdinand of Austria is assassinated. This starts World War I
1916	Battle of the Somme killed about 60,000 soldiers in just one day
1916	The Easter Rising, Irish Nationalist rise against the British in Dublin
1918	At 11.00 am on the 11th November, the war ends with victory for Britain and allies
1921	Peace treaty for Ireland
1922	Ireland becomes 2 countries. Northern Ireland is created. The rest of Ireland becomes a free state

Revision notes - Key Dates

1922	First BBC radio broadcast
1929	Great Depression: mass unemployment
1933	Hitler comes to power in Germany
1936	First BBC Television broadcast
1939	Germany invades Poland. The UK and France declare wars on Germany. This starts World War II
1940	German forces win over the allies and advance through France. Churchill becomes Prime Minister. Dunkirk operation where the Navy rescues more than 300,000 men from beaches in France. Creates the "Dunkirk Spirit" The Battle of Britain is fought in the air to prevent German invasion
1941	Germany invades the Soviet Union The Japanese attack Pearl Harbour in the US. The USA join the allied forces and the war becomes fully global
1944	6 June: the allied forces land in French Normandy (the D-Day) and start repelling the German.
1945	Germany is defeated by the allies. 8 May: Victory in Europe and Germany surrenders August: The US drop 2 atomic bombs over Japanese cities, Hiroshima and Nagasaki to end the war. A Labour government is elected. Clement Attlee becomes Prime Minister
1947	Several countries gain independence from the British Empire: India, Pakistan, Ceylon
1948	The Minister the Health Aneurin Bevan creates the National Health Service (NHS)
1949	Ireland becomes a republic with its own government
1951	Churchill becomes Prime Minister again
1950s	Shortage of labour leads to vast immigration
1957	The European Economic Community is formed by Germany, France, Italy, Belgium, Luxemburg and the Netherlands.

Revision notes - Key Dates

1960s	The Swinging Sixties are a period of social changes., many laws are liberalised (divorce and abortion). Women's position in the workplace improves Technological progress. France and the UK develop a supersonic airliner called Concorde. Immigration laws are enforced to reduce flows.
1970s	End of prosperity. Imports become more expensive than exports. Difficulties between Trade Unions and government.
1972	Northern Ireland Parliament is suspended and the UK government rules over the country. Unrest and violence in Ireland lasts several decades
1973	The UK joins the European Economic Community
1997	Tony Blair is elected Labour Prime Minister
1998	The Good Friday Agreement restores peace in Ireland
1999	Welsh Assembly and a Scottish Parliament are created
2000-2009	British troops fight in Iraq alongside the USA.
2010	A coalition government is formed by the Conservatives and the Liberal Democrats. David Cameron is Prime Minister and Nick Clegg his deputy
2015	The conservative win the elections and David Cameron remain Prime minster
2016	Following a referendum to leave the European Union, David Cameron resigns and Theresa May becomes Prime Minister
2017	The UK will trigger article 50 of the Treaty of Lisbon to initiate its departure from the European Union.

Important people

The six wives of Henry VIII:
- Catherine of Aragon – Spanish princess. One children survived: Mary. Henry divorced her, leading to a split with the Catholic Church
- Anne Boleyn – English. They have one daughter, Elizabeth. Accused of cheating, she was executed.
- Jane Seymour – English. They have a son: Edward. She died shortly after his birth
- Anne of Cleves – German princess. Political marriage that didn't last.
- Catherine Howard – Cousin of Anne Boleyn. Also accused of cheating and executed.
- Catherine Parr – Widow. Died shortly after Henry

William Shakespeare (1564 – 1616)
Born in Stratford-Upon-Avon. Playwright and actor, famous for many plays including *Romeo and Juliet, Hamlet, Macbeth, A Midsummer's night dream*. He largely influenced English language and invented many words (critic, lonely, swager, unearthly, unreal, etc.)

Isaac Newton (1643-1727)
Born in Lincolnshire, studied at Cambridge University. Scientist famous for his book *Philosophiae Naturalis Principia Mathematica* which demonstrated the laws of gravity.

Robert Burns (1759-1796)
A Scottish poet known as 'The Bard' who wrote in Scots. Famous song: *Auld Lang Syne*.

Richard Arkwright (1732-1792)
Trained as a barber and started to work in textiles. He improved the machine that prepares fibres and developed a horse-driven spinning mill before replacing horses with a steam engine. He is famous for running efficient and profitable factories.

Sake Dean Mahomet (1759-1851)
Born in Bengal, India. He served the Bengal army and moved to Britain in 1782. He's famous for opening the first curry house in London and for introducing shampooing to Britain.

Isambard Kingdom Brunel (1806-1859)
Born in Portsmouth, trained in France, he was an engineer. Famous for building the Great Western Railway as well as many bridges, tunnels and ships.

Florence Nightingale (1820-1910)
Born in Italy, trained as a nurse, she went to work in Turkish hospitals during the Crimean war. She is famous for improving the conditions in hospitals and creating training schools for nurses at St Thomas' Hospital in London.

Emmeline Pankhurst (1858-1928)
Born in Manchester, she set up the Women's Franchise League in 1889 to fight for women's right to vote. She founded the women's Social and Political Union (WSPU) also called the suffragettes. In 1918, they won the right to vote for women over 30.

Revision notes - Important people

Rudyard Kipling (1865-1936)
Born in India, he wrote poems and books. Most famous for the Jungle Book and the poem If. He won the Noble prize for literature in 1907.

Winston Churchill (1874-1965)
Became a Conservative MP in 1900. In May 1940 he became Prime Minister and lead the country through World War II. He came back as PM in 1951. He was given state funeral and was voted greatest Briton by the public in 2002.

Alexander Fleming (1881-1955)
Born in Scotland and moved to London as a teenager. Trained as a doctor and researched influenza (the Flu). Famous for discovering penicillin in 1928. He won the Nobel prize for Medicine in 1945.

Clement Attlee (1883-1967)
Born in London, he studied in Oxford University to become a barrister. He became Labour MP and was Churchill deputy during the war. He formed a government in 1945 and oversaw nationalisation of major industries, the creation of the NHS, the implementation of a welfare system and improvement of workers conditions.

William Beveridge (1879-1963)
British economist who served as an MP as well. He is famous for his report in social insurance and allied services that provided the basis for the welfare system.

Richard Austen Butler (1902-1982)
Became conservative MP in 1923 and Minister for Education in 1941. He introduced free secondary education in England and Wales.

Dylan Thomas (1914-1953)
Welsh poet and writer most known for his play Under Milk Wood and the poem Do Not Go Gentle Into That Good Night

Mary Peters (1939-)
Born in Manchester and moved to Northern Ireland as a kid. Talented athlete she won an Olympic Gold Medal in Pentathlon in 1972. She raised money for athletics and became the women's British Olympic Team manager. She promotes sport in Northern Ireland and became a Dame of the British Empire in 2000.

Roald Dahl (1916-1990)
Welsh author. He served in the Royal Air force during World War II. Published many stories for kids including George's Marvellous medicine and Charlie and the Chocolate Factory.

UK population

Evolution of British population through the centuries:

Year	Population
1600	4 million
1700	5 million
1801	8 million
1851	20 million
1901	40 million
1951	50 million
1998	57 million
2005	Just under 60 million
2010	Just over 62 million
2019	Over 66.5 million

The population is ageing. There are now a record number of people aged 85 and over.

Official style tests

In this chapter, you can put your fresh knowledge to the test. You will find 12 complete tests, each made of 24 questions. The answers can be found at the end of each test. The format is the same as you will find during the real test.

A good way to practice is to monitor yourself to ensure you answer every full test in under 45 minutes.

TEST 1

1. Which flag has a white cross on a blue background?

A. Scottish

B. English

C. Welsh

D. Irish

2. Where is the Cenotaph located?

A. Dorset

B. Trafalgar Square

C. Whitehall

D. Wiltshire

3. Who is Queen Elizabeth II married to?

A. Prince William

B. Prince Philip

C. Prince Charles

D. Prince Albert

4. Hanukkah is celebrated to remember the Jews' struggle for religious freedom and it is in November or December for how many days?

A. 6

B. 7

C. 8

D. 9

5. What will happen to any driver who has either taken more than the acceptable quantity of alcohol or refuse to take the test?

A. Taken home

B. Arrested

C. Given a warning

D. Asked to provide medical certificate

Test 1

6. English laws and the English language were introduced in Wales by the middle of which century?

A. 12th Century
B. 13th Century
C. 14th Century
D. 15th Century

7. Which TWO records tell us about England during the time of William I?

A. Magna Carta
B. Canterbury Tales
C. Bayeux Tapestry
D. Doomsday Book

8. King Edward I of England annexed Wales to the crown of England by which statute?

A. Statute of Cardiff
B. Statute of Carmarthen
C. Statute of Gwynedd
D. Statute of Rhuddlan

9. Which of the following statements is correct?

A. The first person to use the title Prime Minister was Sir Christopher Wren
B. The first person to use the title Prime Minister was Sir Robert Walpole

10. Who were the Jutes, Angles and Saxons?

A. Tribespeople from Northern Europe
B. Romans
C. Tribespeople from India
D. Tribespeople from Eastern Europe

11. Which TWO points about slavery are correct?

A. Slavery survived in the British Empire until the early 20th Century
B. Quakers set up the first anti-slavery groups
C. William Wilberforce was a leading abolitionist
D. The Royal Navy refused to stop ships carrying slaves

12. Which of the following statements is correct

A. Police and Crime Commissioners (PCCs) are appointed by the local council.

B. Police and Crime Commissioners (PCCs) are appointed through a public election.

13. Is the following statement TRUE or FALSE?

The 100 days before Easter are known as Lent. It is a time when Christians take time to reflect and prepare for Easter. Traditionally, people would fast during this period.

A. True

B. False

14. Is the statement below TRUE or FALSE?

Rugby originated in England in the early 19th century.

A. True

B. False

15. Who invented the Internet as we know it today? (World Wide Web)

A. Peter Mansfield

B. Sir Tim Berners-Lee

C. Clement Atlee

D. Wilfred Owen

16. Which country's national flower is a thistle?

A. Wales

B. England

C. Scotland

D. Northern Ireland

Test 1

17. Who succeeded Margaret Thatcher as Prime Minister?

A. Kenneth Baker

B. Douglas Hurd

C. John Major

D. Norman Tebbit

18. Is the following statement TRUE or FALSE?

People over 75 can apply for a free TV licence, and blind people can get a 50% discount.

A. True

B. False

19. How old do you have to be to go into betting shops or gambling clubs?

A. 18

B. 20

C. 16

D. 21

20. What is an example of a Criminal Offence?

A. Discrimination in the office

B. Selling tobacco to under 18's

C. Owing money

D. Housing disputes

21. Is the following statement TRUE or FALSE?

The Corn Laws were repealed in 1846. This had prevented the import of cheap grain

A. True

B. False

Test 1

22. Which of these is correct in the chronological order?

A. the Black Death, Canterbury Tales, Magna Carta

B. the Black Death, Magna Carta, Canterbury Tales

C. Canterbury Tales, the Black Death, Magna Carta

D. Magna Carta, the Black Death, Canterbury Tales,

23. What did R. A. Butler introduce?

A. Free secondary education in England

B. Free college education in Scotland

C. Free university education in the UK

D. Free primary education in Wales

24. Who directed the two British films 'Brief Encounter' and 'Lawrence of Arabia'?

A. Hugh Hundson

B. Alfred Hitchcock

C. David Lean

D. William Walton

1. A – 2.C – 3.B – 4.C – 5.B – 6.D – 7.C,D – 8.D – 9.B – 10.A – 11.B,C – 12.B – 13.B – 14.A – 15.B – 16.C – 17.C – 18.A – 19.A – 20.B – 21.A – 22.D – 23.A – 24.C

TEST 2

1. Is the following statement TRUE or FALSE?

The Glorious Revolution was called the "Glorious revolution" because there was no fighting in England and it guaranteed the power of Parliament

A. True

B. False

2. Which TWO are members of Parliament (MPs) responsible for?

A. Representing every person in their constituency

B. Representing the people who voted for them

C. Supporting the government on all laws and decisions

D. Commenting on and challenging what the government is doing.

3. How many members does the Scottish Parliament have?

A. 60

B. 108

C. 129

D. 320

4. Is the following statement TRUE or FALSE?

At its peak the British Empire had an estimated population of just under 400 million.

A. True

B. False

5. There is no place in British society for which TWO of the following?

A. Intolerance

B. Extremism

C. Democracy

D. Politics

Test 2

6. What special type of windows did many cathedrals built in the Middle Ages have?

A. Stained glass

B. Mullioned

C. Sash

D. Arched

7. Who is the longest reigning British monarch?

A. Victoria

B. Henry VIII

C. Elizabeth II

D. Richard II

8. Which TWO of the following are British inventions?

A. Hovercraft

B. Golfcraft

C. Jet Engine

D. Helicopter

9. When did hereditary peers lose the automatic right to attend the House of Lords?

A. 1979

B. 1969

C. 1989

D. 1999

10. Is the following statement TRUE or FALSE?

Mary Queen of Scots was related to Elizabeth I

A. True

B. False

11. In 1913, the British government promised Home Rule for Ireland. Which group within Ireland resisted the move with force?

A. The Catholics in the North

B. The Protestants in the North

C. The Protestants in the South

D. The Catholics in the South

Test 2

12. Which of the following is a British invention or innovation?

A. Micro machines

B. A Turing machine

C. The telephone

D. The photocopier

13. People can be randomly chosen for jury service if they are which TWO of the following?

A. Aged between 18 and 80

B. On the electoral register

C. Aged at least 50

D. A member of the police

14. Is the following statement TRUE or FALSE?

There are 9 National Parks in the UK

A. True

B. False

15. What are the parliaments in Scotland, Wales and Northern Ireland also known as?

A. Formal institutions

B. Political parties

C. Devolved administrations

D. Local authorities

16. EU citizens who are resident in the UK can vote in national parliamentary elections

A. Yes

B. Sometimes

C. No

17. Who was the monarch when the Book of Common Prayer was written to be used in the Church of England?

A. Edward VI

B. Henry VII

C. Henry VIII

D. Richard III

Test 2

18. What percentage of the UK population lives in England?

A. 76%

B. 82%

C. 78%

D. 84%

19. Which of the options given below is not necessary for a new car?

A. Seat belts

B. Car insurance

C. MOT test

D. Road tax

20. What is not a fundamental principle of British life?

A. Driving a car

B. Looking after the environment

C. Looking after yourself and family

D. Treating others with fairness

21. Is the following statement TRUE or FALSE?

Gertrude Jekyll was a famous garden designer.

A. True

B. False

22. The writer Roald Dahl served in the Royal Air Force during which conflict?

A. Second World War

B. The Suez Crisis

C. Korean War

D. First World War

Test 2

23. Is the following statement TRUE or FALSE?

Proceedings in Parliament cannot be reported in press or broadcast on television.

A. True

B. False

24. Which country did Germany invade in 1939 that led to the UK declaring war?

A. Poland

B. France

C. Austria

D. Russia

TEST 3

1. Which of these UK landmarks is in Wales?

A. Loch Lomond

B. The Giant's Causeway

C. The Lake District

D. Snowdonia

2. Is the following statement TRUE or FALSE?

British scientists were the first to clone a mammal successfully.

A. True

B. False

3. Which form of religion developed as a result of the Reformation?

A. Protestantism

B. Methodism

C. Hinduism

D. Baptism

4. When did King Edward I of England introduced the Statute of Rhuddlan by which Wales annexed to the Crown of England?

A. 1284

B. 1200

C. 1743

D. 1812

5. What is the correct name of the film directed by Kevin MacDonald and made in 2003?

A. Touching the Top

B. Touching the Untouchable

C. Touching the Void

D. Touching the Stone

6. Is the following statement TRUE or FALSE?

Women were given the right to vote at the same age as men in 1982

A. True

B. False

7. Which TWO are correct about Mary Stuart?

A. She was a week old when she became queen
B. She died during the Black Death
C. She was Elizabeth I's sister
D. She spent most of her childhood in France

8. What is the only major golf tournament held outside of the US?

A. Royal Ascot
B. The Open Championship
C. Wimbledon
D. The Premier League

9. Is the following statement TRUE or FALSE?

Constituencies which had hardly any voters were called 'Pocket Boroughs'

A. True

B. False

10. Who was the skating partner of Christopher Dean when they won a gold medal in the 1984 Olympic Games?

A. Jayne Torvill
B. Mary Torvill
C. Mary Jayne
D. Katarina Jayne

11. Which of the following areas does civil law cover?

A. Burglary
B. Debt
C. Drunk and disorderly behaviour
D. Violent crime

12. The National Church is the Church of Scotland. What kind of Church is it?

A. Presbyterian
B. Scientologist
C. Amish
D. Mormon

13. What did the Chartists campaign for?

A. The right to vote at 18
B. The right to vote for women
C. The right to vote for the working class
D. The right to vote at 21

14. Which Two British film actors have won Oscars?

A. Tilda Swinton
B. Colin firth
C. Leonardo DiCaprio
D. Jacky Stewart

15. Which event occurs each year on the third Sunday in June?

A. Halloween
B. Father's Day
C. Mother's Day
D. Easter Sunday

16. Which of the following statements is correct?

A. The Wars of the Roses were between the Houses of Lancaster and York
B. The Wars of the Roses were between the Houses of Windsor and Tudor

17. Is the following statement TRUE or FALSE?

England, Scotland, Wales and Northern Ireland are governed only by the parliament sitting in Westminster.

A. True
B. False

18. In what English county can you see the hill fort at Maiden Castle?

A. Cornwall

B. Dorset

C. East Lothian

D. Danebury

19. How many Olympic gold medals has the Scottish cyclist, Sir Chris Hoy, won?

A. 7

B. 6

C. 2

D. 5

20. Rudyard Kipling was awarded which major prize in 1907?

A. The Pulitzer prize

B. The Somerset Maugham prize

C. The Nobel prize

D. The Man Booker prize

21. Which of the following statements is correct?

A. After the election of a Conservative government in 1945, the NHS and a social security system was established.

B. After the election of a Labour government in 1945, the NHS and a social security system was established

22. Where were the first farmers that came to Britain from?

A. North west Europe

B. South west Europe

C. North Europe

D. South east Europe

23. William Beveridge (later Lord Beveridge) was a British economist and social reformer. Which political party was he the leader of?

A. The Conservative Party

B. The Liberal Party

C. The Labour Party

D. The Green Party

24. Which TWO are Protestant Christian groups in the UK?

A. Baptists

B. Methodists

C. Roman Catholics

D. Hindus

TEST 4

1. After the Black Death, a new social class appeared, – owners of large areas of land. What were they called?

A. The Tudors

B. The Gentry

C. The Serfs

D. The Clans

2. Which TWO of these literary pieces are the work of Welsh poet and writer Dylan Thomas, who lived from 1914 until his death in New York in 1953?

A. Brave New World

B. Under Milk Wood

C. Nineteen Eighty-Four

D. Do Not Go Gentle Into That Good Night

3. What method is used to elect UK MPs?

A. Proportional Representation

B. Popularity

C. Instant runoff

D. First past the post system

4. What party won the election in 1945 (After WWII)?

A. Conservative

B. Liberal Democrats

C. Labour

D. A coalition

5. Which country did NOT gain its independence from the British Empire in 1947?

A. India

B. Pakistan

C. Sri Lanka

D. The Caribbean

Test 4

6. Is the following statement TRUE or FALSE?

Police forces are independent of the government.

A. True

B. False

7. When did the American Colonies declare their independence?

A. 1776

B. 1733

C. 1749

D. 1783

8. Who discovered Insulin?

A. John MacLeod

B. Mary Peters

C. Patrick Steptoe

D. Ian Wilmot

9. Which ship was one of the first to sail around the world?

A. Golden Hind

B. HMS Victory

C. The Ship of Royals

D. Royal Yacht Britannia

10. Which charity works to preserve important buildings?

A. NSPCC

B. Age UK

C. The Red Cross

D. The National Trust

11. When is St David's day?

A. 17th of March

B. 23rd of April

C. 1st of March

D. 30th of November

Test 4

12. Which of the following is the St Patron of Scotland:

A. St David

B. St Patrick

C. St George

D. St Andrew

13. Who was the first Briton to win the Olympic gold medal in the 10,000 meters?

A. Bradley Wiggins

B. Mo Farah

C. Sir Chris Hoy

D. David Weir

14. What created the United Kingdom of Great Britain and Ireland?

A. The Great Union

B. The Act of Union

C. The Act of the governments

D. The Great governments

15. Which of the following statements is correct?

A. County Courts deal with criminal cases

B. County Courts deal with civil disputes

16. Following the Bill of Rights, for which TWO are monarchs required to ask Parliament to renew funding for each year?

A. Army

B. Navy

C. Castles

D. Palaces

17. Where was Robert Burns from?

A. England

B. Northern Ireland

C. Wales

D. Scotland

18. Which British inventor was responsible for developing the television in the 1920s?

A. John Logie Baird
B. Sir Robert Watson-Watt
C. Sir Bernard Lovell
D. John Macleod

19. Is the following statement TRUE or FALSE?

The European Convention on Human Rights is incorporated into UK law

A. True
B. False

20. Where is the best preserved prehistoric village "Skara Brae on Orkney" located?

A. England
B. Scotland
C. Wales
D. Ireland

21. Who was John Constable?

A. A landscape painter, most famous for his works of Dedham Vale on the Suffolk-Essex border in the East of England
B. An important contributor to the 'pop art' movement of the 1960s
C. A Welsh artist, best known for his engravings and stained glass
D. A very successful Northern Irish portrait painter

22. Which flower is associated with England?

A. Rose
B. Daffodil
C. Thistle
D. Shamrock

23. Geoffrey Chaucer is associated with which of the following stories?

A. The London Tales

B. The Kent Tales

C. The Reading Tales

D. The Canterbury Tales

24. Who built the Tower of London?

A. Oliver Cromwell

B. Elizabeth I

C. Henry VIII

D. William the Conqueror

TEST 5

1. Is the following statement TRUE or FALSE?

There are charities which may help people who cannot afford to pay a vet.

A. True

B. False

2. What is the capital of Wales?

A. Belfast

B. Cardiff

C. Edinburgh

D. Swansea

3. Is the following statement TRUE or FALSE?

The 'plantation' settlements in Ireland during the 17th century led to Catholic farmers replacing Protestant landowners.

A. True

B. False

4. Which of the following jobs is usually unpaid in England, Wales and Scotland?

A. Wardens

B. Magistrates and Justices of the Peace

C. Civil lawyers

D. Policeman

5. What service does the TV licence pay for?

A. Freeview channels

B. The BBC

C. Free radio and TV channels

D. None of these

Test 5

6. Dylan Thomas was a famous writer and poet from which country?

A. England

B. Northern Ireland

C. Wales

D. Scotland

7. Is the following statement TRUE or FALSE?

The Prime Minister is the head of the Commonwealth

A. True

B. False

8. What Palace was a cast-iron and plate-glass building originally erected in Hyde Park, London, England, to house the Great Exhibition of 1851?

A. Crystal Palace

B. Gold Palace

C. the Great Palace

D. Dream Palace.

9. Is the following statement TRUE or FALSE?

It is legal to send a girl abroad for circumcision or cutting.

A. True

B. False

10. On St David's Day in Wales, which flower would you expect to see people wearing?

A. Rose

B. Sunflower

C. Daffodil

D. Poppy

11. Which of the following statements is correct?

A. The civil service largely consists of political appointees

B. The civil service is politically neutral

12. When is the public holiday, Boxing Day?

A. The Sunday two weeks before Easter
B. The Friday of the Christmas weekend
C. The day after New Year's day
D. The day after Christmas day

13. Is the following statement TRUE or FALSE?

In the year 1588 the English defeated the Spanish Armada

A. True
B. False

14. Where can you get details about the small claims procedure?

A. Your local polling station
B. Your local County Court
C. Any council
D. The High Court

15. In which year did Margaret thatcher became Member of Parliament?

A. 1949
B. 1959
C. 1979
D. 1989

16. Which TWO materials did the UK produce more than half of the world production in the 19th century?

A. Iron
B. Bronze
C. Potatoes
D. Cotton Cloth

17. What is the name given to the conflict between those wishing for full Irish independence and those wishing to remain loyal to the UK government?

A. The Troubles
B. The Great Depression
C. The Problems
D. The Clearances

18. Which TWO of the following are major horse-racing events in the UK?

A. Royal Ascot
B. The Grand National
C. Champions League
D. Wimbledon

19. Which of the following statements is correct?

A. Members of the public are not allowed to attend Youth Court hearings.
B. Members of the public are allowed to attend Youth Court hearings.

20. Which organization looks after the Edinburgh Castle?

A. The National Trust
B. NSPCC
C. Historic Scotland
D. The Red Cross

21. When did the Vikings first attack Britain?

A. AD 798
B. AD 789
C. AD 879
D. AD 897

22. Who captained the English football team in 1966?

A. Sir Chris Hoy
B. Bobby Moore
C. Andy Murray
D. Jackie Stewart

23. Where are the more serious civil cases dealt with in Scotland?

A. Court of Session
B. High Court
C. Peace Courts
D. Sheriff Court

Test 5

24. Which of the following is a modern British architect?

A. Dame Zaha Hadid

B. Thomas Chippendale

C. Dame Ellen MacArthur

D. Sir William Golding

TEST 6

1. Which TWO are British Overseas Territories?

A. Ireland

B. The Falkland Islands

C. St Helena

D. Hawaii

2. Who was Henry Purcell?

A. A gardener

B. An actor

C. A musician

D. A poet

3. What is known as Lent?

A. The 40 days after Easter

B. The 40 days before Easter

C. The 40 days before Christmas

D. The 40 days after Christmas

4. Which TWO of the following do lobby and pressure groups do?

A. Influence government policy

B. Represent views of British businesses

C. Organise protests

D. Vote the laws

5. Is the following statement TRUE or FALSE?

The British constitution is contained in a single written document.

A. False

B. True

Test 6

6. Is the following statement TRUE or FALSE?
The small claims procedure is an informal way of helping people to settle minor disputes.

A. True

B. False

7. Is the following statement TRUE or FALSE?
Most shops in the UK open seven days a week.

A. True

B. False

8. For how many years did the Romans approximately stay in this country?

A. 400

B. 100

C. 200

D. 1000

9. Which TWO of the following are major outdoor music festivals?

A. Glastonbury

B. Isle of Wight Festival

C. Royal Ascot

D. The Grand National

10. What were TWO important aspects of the Reform Act of 1832?

A. It increases the number of people who could vote

B. It abolished slavery

C. It gave women the right to vote

D. It abolished rotten boroughs

11. Is the following statement TRUE or FALSE?
The UK has a declining elderly population.

A. True

B. False

12. What were 'the Troubles' about?

A. Disagreement about Ireland becoming one country

B. Independence for Scotland

C. Reducing power over the monarch

D. Independence for Wales

13. Which TWO of the following must you pay tax on?

A. Shopping vouchers

B. Profits from self-employment

C. Family gifts

D. Revenue from dividends

14. Which TWO types of case can be held in County Courts?

A. Divorce

B. Trafficking

C. Murder

D. Breaches of contract

15. For UK citizens and permanent residents, what TWO freedoms are offered?

A. Free utility supply

B. Leaving work early on Friday

C. A right to a fair trial

D. Freedom of speech

16. In order to vote in elections what must you have done

A. Have your name on the electoral register

B. Paid your income tax for the previous year

C. Registered with your local council

D. Pass an electoral test

17. What is the monarch's ceremonial role?

A. Going abroad

B. Travelling in the UK

C. Opening a parliamentary session

D. Making policies

Test 6

18. Where does the Prime Minister reside?

A. The Buckingham Palace

B. 76 Charlotte Street

C. 10 Downing Street

D. 1 Devonshire Terrace

19. What system automatically deducts tax from salary?

A. HMRC

B. PAYE

C. Self-Assessment

D. PAYG

20. What was the population of the UK in 1901?

A. 50 million

B. 40 million

C. 60 million

D. 27 million

21. What programme helps teenagers develop their skills?

A. The National Citizen Service

B. The Teenage Programme

C. The Youth Development Service

D. Youth Opportunities

22. What is the role of the Opposition in parliament?

A. To participate in public debates

B. To represent the people of the UK

C. To challenge the government

D. To change laws

23. How often do you have to take a MOT test for an old vehicle?

A. Every year

B. Every 2 years

C. Every 3 years

D. Every 4 years

Test 6

24. Where does the Scottish Grand National take place?

A. Aintree

B. Edinburgh

C. Ayr

D. Berkshire

TEST 7

1. Who won the Tour de France?

A. Sir Chris Hoy

B. Bradley Wiggins

C. Mo Farah

D. Andy Murray

2. Who created James Bond?

A. Ian Fleming

B. JRR Tolkien

C. William Golding

D. J K Rowling

3. Which of these is not a valid bank note?

A. £5

B. £15

C. £20

D. £10

4. Which TWO new national bodies were established in 1999?

A. Welsh Assembly

B. Scottish Parliament

C. Irish Assembly

D. Northern Ireland Assembly

5. On the 5th of November what event is remembered each year?

A. Thanksgiving

B. The Queen's Birthday

C. Halloween

D. A plot by Guy Fawkes to blow up the Houses of Parliament

6. Which TWO of the following are Christian religious festivals that are celebrated in the UK?

A. Christmas

B. May Day

C. Halloween

D. Easter

7. Is the following statement TRUE or FALSE?

The UK is governed by the parliament sitting in Westminster.

A. False

B. True

8. What government type was formed after the General Election in 2010?

A. Two-party

B. Bi-party

C. National

D. Coalition

9. Which of the following is the name of a novel by Jane Austen?

A. Oliver Twist

B. Sense and Sensibility

C. The Lord of the Flies

D. Great Expectations

10. Which of the following is a famous Stone Age site in the UK?

A. Trafalgar Square

B. Globe Theatre

C. Stonehenge

D. Buckingham Palace

11. Is the following statement TRUE or FALSE?

Florence Nightingale (1820–1910) was famous for her work to improve the quality of nursing and hospital conditions.

A. True

B. False

Test 7

12. Where is the National Assembly for Wales based?

A. London

B. Cardiff

C. Edinburgh

D. Newport

13. Is the following statement TRUE or FALSE?

If your driving licence is from a country in the European Union you have to apply for a UK licence in order to drive.

A. True

B. False

14. During the English Civil War, which TWO were associated with King Charles I and Parliament?

A. Tories

B. Labour

C. Cavaliers

D. Roundheads

15. Which TWO are examples of civil law?

A. Housing disputes

B. Carrying firearms

C. Selling alcohol without a licence

D. Employment discrimination

16. What county does Stonehenge stand in?

A. Berkshire

B. Wiltshire

C. Lancashire

D. Lothians

17. When were the last Welsh rebellions defeated?

A. 16th Century

B. 15th Century

C. 14th Century

D. 17th Century

18. When was the time of growing patriotism?

A. The Golden Age
B. The Iron Age
C. The Elizabethan period
D. The Victorian Age

19. How many national parks are there in the UK?

A. 15
B. 25
C. 10
D. 20

20. How are local councils funded?

A. Through local taxes and central government
B. From tax on local businesses
C. From local donations
D. From fundraising

21. Is the following statement TRUE or FALSE?

Members of the public can attend Youth Court hearings.

A. True
B. False

22. Which TWO are famous UK landmarks?

A. Loch Lomond
B. Snowdonia
C. Yellowstone Park
D. Eiffel Tower

23. Who founded a monastery on the Island of Iona?

A. St Patrick
B. St David
C. St Columba
D. St Augustine

Test 7

24. Which political party is still known as the Tories?

A. Labour

B. Conservative

C. Liberal Democrats

D. British National Party

1.B – 2.A – 3.B – 4.A,B – 5.D – 6.A,D – 7.A – 8.D – 9.B – 10.C – 11.A – 12.B – 13.B – 14.C,D – 15.A,D – 16.B – 17.B – 18.C – 19.A – 20.A – 21.B – 22.A,B – 23.C – 24.B

TEST 8

1. Who developed ideas about economics which are still referred to today?

A. James Watt

B. David Hume

C. Adam Smith

D. Isaac Newton

2. Is the following statement TRUE or FALSE?

One TV licence covers all of the equipment at one address, but people who rent different rooms in a shared house must buy a separate TV licence

A. True

B. False

3. What group of refugees came to settle in England between 1680 and 1720?

A. Scottish

B. Indians

C. Scandinavian

D. Huguenots

4. Ted Hughes and John Masefield are both famous as what?

A. Actors

B. Poets

C. Dancers

D. Fighters

5. Which TWO major welfare changes were introduced between 1945 and 1950?

A. The NHS

B. A social security system for everyone

C. Employments benefits

D. State pension

6. Is the following statement TRUE or FALSE?

EastEnders and Coronation Street are popular TV shows

A. True

B. False

7. The Scottish Parliament

A. May pass laws on foreign and defence affairs

B. May pass laws on general economic policy

C. Is not elected by a form of proportional representation

D. May pass legislation on anything not specifically reserved to the UK Parliament

8. Which of these countries was part of the British Empire during Victoria's reign?

A. France

B. USA

C. India

D. Germany

9. What happened in 1918 to make it an important date in the history of women's rights?

A. Wives were given the right to keep their own earnings

B. Women were given the right to vote

C. Women were made legally responsible for their children's crime

D. Equal pay laws were passed

10. Which famous British novelist wrote Brighton Rock?

A. William Golding

B. Arthur Conan Doyle

C. Graham Greene

D. William Worstworth

11. Civil Servants are accountable to

A. Members of Parliament

B. Ministers

C. The national party

D. the Queen

12. Which of these birds is traditionally associated with Christmas in the UK?

A. Chicken

B. Swan

C. Turkey

D. Pigeon

13. English kings fought a long war with France wich was known as:

A. The English War

B. The Ten Year War

C. The French War

D. The Hundred Year War

14. Who invaded the Falkland Islands in 1982?

A. Spain

B. Argentina

C. Portugal

D. Columbia

15. After drivers reach 70 years old, their driving licence is valid for how many years?

A. 1

B. 2

C. 3

D. 4

16. Is the following statement TRUE or FALSE?

The Scottish Parliament building opened in October 2004.

A. True

B. False

17. Where did Charles II hide to escape from Cromwell's army?

A. In a house attic

B. In a church

C. In an oak tree

D. In a garden

Test 8

18. Whose approval Henry the VIII needed to divorce his first wife?

A. The Archbishop of Canterbury

B. The king of France

C. Parliament

D. The pope

19. The UK belongs to which TWO international bodies?

A. The North Atlantic Free Trade Agreement (NAFTA)

B. The North Atlantic Treaty Organization (NATO)

C. The Commonwealth

D. Collective Security Treaty Organization (CSTO)

20. What medal was introduced during the Crimean War?

A. The Medal of Honour

B. The Victoria Cross

C. Elizabeth gold

D. The Elizabeth Medal

21. Which charity is working with older people

A. Age UK

B. NSPCC

C. The Red Cross

D. National Trust

22. William III of England, Wales and Ireland was which king of Scotland?

A. William IV

B. William II

C. William I

D. William III

23. Which of the following is a document or piece of legislation that sets out fundamental rights or freedoms?

A. The Habeas Corpus Act

B. The UK Constitution

C. the Act of Union

D. The Statute of Rhuddlan

24. What was encouraged to develop the UK economy in 1950?

A. Education

B. Slave Trade

C. Immigration

D. Savings Accounts

TEST 9

1. Which TWO are required for people to be randomly selected for jury service?

A. Aged at least 16

B. Aged between 18 and 70

C. Be on the electoral register

D. Be on the jury register

2. Why did the Roman Emperor Hadrian build a wall across parts of northern England?

A. To form settlements

B. To keep out the Picts

C. To keep out the Normans

D. To prevent theft of his livestock

3. The Welsh government and National Assembly for Wales are based in

A. Newport

B. Cardiff

C. Bangor

D. Swansea

4. Who designed New Delhi to be the seat of government in India?

A. Sir Edwin Lutyens

B. Sir Christopher Wren

C. Inigo jones

D. Robert Adam

5. When did William of Orange invade England?

A. 1692

B. 1688

C. 1684

D. 1696

6. Which of the following is a famous British film?

A. Passport to Paddington

B. Passport to Pimlico

C. Passport to Panama

D. Passport to Portsmouth

7. When did the "Battle of Agincourt" take place?

A. 1200

B. 1613

C. 1415

D. 1716

8. Who did Henry VII marry to form an alliance?

A. Elizabeth Tudor

B. Elizabeth of York

C. Elizabeth of Lancaster

D. Catherine of Aragon

9. When did Queen Elizabeth II celebrate her Diamond Jubilee?

A. 2011

B. 2012

C. 2013

D. 2014

10. What is Diwali popularly known as?

A. The Festival of Fireworks

B. The Festival of Darkness

C. The Festival of Lights

D. The Festival of Colours

11. What was the name of plague that killed one third of the population of England in 1348?

A. The White Death

B. The Pig Flu

C. The Bird Flu

D. The Black Death

12. When was The National Trust founded?

A. 1945
B. 1789
C. 1895
D. 1845

13. Where can you find a solicitor in the UK?

A. The Citizen Advice Bureau
B. A police station
C. In a Youth Court
D. In a law firm

14. Is the following statement TRUE or FALSE?

Mothering Sunday is two weeks before Easter

A. True
B. False

15. Which of these is NOT a city in the UK?

A. Leeds
B. Brussels
C. Bradford
D. Blackpool

16. Do magistrates need legal qualifications?

A. Yes
B. No

17. Which play was written by Shakespeare

A. Hamlet
B. Before the Dawn
C. Freedom of Love
D. Come, walk with me

18. What is Yorkshire pudding?

A. Batter cooked in the oven

B. A dessert made with raisins and dates

C. A pastry filled with meet and potato

D. Bacon, Eggs and sausage

19. What was an important English export in the middle ages?

A. Glass

B. Wool

C. Potatoes

D. Stone

20. Which of the following is the fastest person to have sailed around the world, single-handed?

A. Dame Mary Peters

B. Dame Ellen MacArthur

C. Dame Agatha Christie

D. Dame Kelly Holmes

21. Women received the right to vote at the same age as men in

A. 1918

B. 1928

C. 1938

D. 1948

22. Where was the Battle of Britain fought?

A. Air

B. Land

C. Sea

D. Underground

23. Which industry has an annual event that gives out Brit awards?

A. Radio

B. Film

C. Sport

D. Music

Test 9

24. If you watch TV without a licence you will receive a fine of up to...

A. £200

B. £400

C. £500

D. £1000

1.B,C – 2.B – 3.B – 4.A – 5.B – 6.B – 7.C – 8.B – 9.B – 10.C – 11.D – 12.C – 13.A – 14.A – 15.B – 16.B – 17.A – 18.A – 19.C – 20.B – 21.B – 22.A – 23.D – 24.D

TEST 10

1. What nationality is Sir Robert Watson-Watt, who developed radar in the 1930s?

A. English

B. Scottish

C. Welsh

D. Irish

2. The day before Lent starts is called

A. Boxing Day

B. Good Friday

C. Shrove Tuesday

D. April Fool's Day

3. Ministers form the Cabinet, a committee which meets every:

A. Day

B. Week

C. Fortnight

D. Month

4. Who became one of the most popular monarchs in the 16th century?

A. Henry VIII

B. Henry VII

C. Elizabeth I

D. Mary I

5. The Book of Common Prayer was introduced during the reign of which monarch?

A. Henry VIII

B. Edward VI

C. Elizabeth I

D. King Richard III

6. Is the following statement TRUE or FALSE?

D-Day is the day when the British landed on the French coast in Normandy.

A. True

B. False

7. Is the following statement TRUE or FALSE?

The Scottish Parliament building opened in October 2004.

A. True

B. False

8. Is the following statement TRUE or FALSE?

Rugby was born in England in the 19th Century

A. True

B. False

9. Devolved administrations in the UK have power other which?

A. Education

B. Defence

C. Immigration

D. Foreign Affair

10. The Wars of the Roses were fought between which TWO houses?

A. House of Wessex

B. House of York

C. House of Lancaster

D. House of Sussex

11. How many years did the Romans remain in Britain?

A. 100

B. 200

C. 300

D. 400

12. When is Bonfire night celebrated?

A. April 1st

B. May 29th

C. November 5th

D. December 25th

13. The first people lived in Britain during which period?

A. The Steel Age

B. The bronze Age

C. The Rock Age

D. The Stone Age

14. What's the age requirement to drink wine with a meal when accompanied with someone over 18?

A. 16

B. 17

C. 18

D. 21

15. Catherine of Aragon, wife of Henry VIII was a princess from which country?

A. England

B. Spain

C. France

D. Wales

16. Who became the first Archbishop of Canterbury?

A. St Columba

B. St George

C. St Augustine

D. St Patrick

17. When is Halloween celebrated?

A. 31 October

B. 30 November

C. 30 October

D. 31 November

Test 10

18. Where is the Royal Crescent located?

A. London

B. Bath

C. Cardiff

D. Edinburgh

19. How long does Diwali normally last for?

A. 5 days

B. 8 days

C. 7 days

D. 10 days

20. Who are TWO famous Paralympians?

A. Dame Ellen MacArthur

B. Ellie Simmonds

C. Baroness Tanni Grey-Thompson

D. Jessica Ennis

21. The Speaker of the House of Commons is chosen by

A. The Prime Minister

B. By the monarch

C. By the public

D. Through a secret ballot

22. Is the following statement TRUE or FALSE?

Bishops of the Church of England are allowed to sit in the House of Lords.

A. True

B. False

23. After the abolition of slavery in 1833, migrants came from which country to replace slaves?

A. Australia

B. France

C. China

D. Russia

24. What is the Giant's Causeway made of?

A. Stone

B. Bronze

C. Marble

D. Volcanic Lava

TEST 11

1. Which of the following is a fundamental principle of British life?

A. Communism

B. Intolerance

C. Individual liberty

D. Inequity

2. Who wrote Sherlock Holmes?

A. Evelyn Waugh

B. Sir Kingsley Amis

C. Graham Greene

D. Sir Arthur Conan Doyle

3. Who was the leader of the suffragettes, the group that campaigned for women's rights to vote?

A. Queen Victoria

B. Oliver Cromwell

C. Florence Nightingale

D. Emmeline Pankhurst

4. What medal did Mary Peters win in the 1972 Olympics?

A. She did not win any medals

B. Silver

C. Gold

D. Bronze

5. What was the religion of the Puritans?

A. Hindu

B. Catholic

C. Sikh

D. Protestant

Test 11

6. When did the Emancipation Act abolish slavery throughout the British Empire?

A. 1835

B. 1823

C. 1807

D. 1833

7. What was achieved with the Magna Carta?

A. It restricted the King's power

B. It increased the King's power

C. It restricted the rights of the farmers

D. It increased women's power

8. What is the judiciary responsible for?

A. Interpreting the law

B. Deciding whether a person is guilty

C. Putting people in prison

D. Looking after a jury

9. What took place in Dunkirk that gave rise to the "Dunkirk spirit"?

A. When the German air force bombed London and other British cities at night-time

B. The evacuation of Allied soldiers from France during World War II

C. When new social classes appeared after the Black Death

D. The period when many refugees called Huguenots came from France

10. Which of the following statements is true?

A. Women in Britain today make up about half of the workforce.

B. Women in Britain today make up about one quarter of the workforce.

11. What type of literature are the Canterbury Tales?

A. Poems

B. Novels

C. Jokes

D. Fables

Test 11

12. What charity works to preserve important buildings, coastline and countryside in the UK?

A. Shelter

B. Age UK

C. Crisis

D. The National Trust

13. Which two houses form the UK Parliament?

A. The House of Lords

B. House of Members

C. House of Commons

D. House of Fraser

14. How many member states does the Commonwealth have?

A. 5

B. 27

C. 38

D. 54

15. When is Hogmanay celebrated?

A. 25th of December

B. 2nd of January

C. 1st of January

D. 31st of December

16. Who was the tribal leader who fought against the Romans?

A. Columba

B. Claudius

C. Hadrian

D. Boudicca

17. Why were canals built during the Industrial Revolution?

A. To link the factories to towns and cities and to the ports

B. To make space for the large fleet of British ships

C. To increase the number of water mills in the UK

D. To increase the amount of water in towns and cities

18. Which of the following is a rugby competition?

A. The Scottish Grand National
B. The Wimbledon Championships
C. The Ashes
D. The Six Nations Championship

19. Where do Beefeaters serve as tour guides?

A. The Houses of the Parliament
B. The Tower of London
C. The O2
D. The Big Ben

20. Who is the spiritual leader of the Church of England?

A. The Archbishop of Canterbury
B. The Archbishop of London
C. The Archbishop of Birmingham
D. The Archbishop of Manchester

21. Who defeated the Vikings?

A. Harold
B. Edward I of England
C. King Arthur
D. King Alfred the Great

22. Is the following statement TRUE or FALSE?

In the UK, you have to be 21 years old to be able to vote in a general election.

A. True
B. False

23. What was Edward Elgar famous for?

A. He was a musician
B. He was a tennis player
C. He was a comedian
D. He was an actor

24. What was Isaac Newton known for?

A. The discovery of insulin

B. The discovery of gravity

C. The discovery of penicillin

D. The discovery of the steam power

TEST 12

1. Who is the patron Saint of England?

A. St George

B. St Patrick

C. St David

D. St Andrew

2. Why were women given the right to vote?

A. In recognition of the contribution women made to the war effort during the First World War

B. In recognition of the contribution women made to the war effort during the Second World War

C. In recognition of the contribution women made to the war effort during the Crimean War

D. In recognition of the contribution women made to the war effort during the Civil War

3. Which two universities participate in an annual rowing race that takes place on the River Thames?

A. The University of Oxford

B. The University of Cambridge

C. The University of Manchester

D. The University of Warwick

4. Which sport can be traced back to the 15th century in Scotland?

A. Golf

B. Tennis

C. Football

D. Rugby

5. How many members does a jury have in England, Wales and Northern Ireland?

A. 9

B. 12

C. 15

D. 20

Test 12

6. What did the Scottish John Logie Baird develop?

A. Television

B. Radar

C. Personal computer

D. Radio

7. What should you do to make a complaint about the police (choose two answers)?

A. Write a complaint letter to the House of Commons

B. Go to the Police station directly

C. Write to the Chief Constable of the police force involved

D. Write to your MP

8. Who did Britain fight against in the Crimean War?

A. Turkey

B. Russia

C. France

D. Germany

9. Which two languages combined to become one English language?

A. Latin

B. Anglo-Saxon

C. Proto-Celtic

D. Norman French

10. What is the name of the holiday when banks and many other businesses are closed for the day?

A. Credit Holidays

B. Branch Holidays

C. Bank Holidays

D. Business Holidays

11. Who built a wall in the north of England to keep out the Picts (ancestors of the Scottish people)?

A. Boudicca

B. Emperor Hadrian

C. Emperor Claudius

D. Julius Caesar

Test 12

12. How many members does the Welsh Assembly have?

A. 150

B. 120

C. 90

D. 60

13. Where does "the Fringe" festival take place?

A. Fraserburgh

B. Edinburgh

C. Inverness

D. St Andrews

14. During the reign of Elizabeth I, a large fleet of ships was sent to England to conquer the country and to restore Catholicism, where did this fleet come from?

A. France

B. Portugal

C. Spain

D. Italy

15. In 1348, a disease, probably a form of plague, came to Britain. What was it called?

A. Malaria

B. White Death

C. Black Death

D. Giant Evil

16. The Victoria Cross medal was introduced during which war?

A. The Hundred Years War

B. The First World War

C. The Crimean War

D. The Second World War

17. What percentage of the total UK population lives in Wales?

A. 5%

B. 3%

C. 1%

D. 8%

Test 12

18. When did English become the official language for documents?

A. 1400

B. 1451

C. 1554

D. 1502

19. Which TWO are famous British fashion designers?

A. Robert Adam

B. Mary Quant

C. Isambard Kingdom Brunel

D. Alexander McQueen

20. During the civil war of 1455, what colour rose was the symbol of the House of Lancaster?

A. Red

B. White

C. Read and White

D. Orange

21. Robert and George Stephenson were famous pioneers of which industry?

A. Railway engines

B. Canal building

C. Agricultural

D. Automobile

22. St Augustine led missionaries from Rome. Where did he spread Christianity?

A. In the East

B. In the West

C. In the South

D. In the North

23. When did motor-car racing start in the UK?

A. 1899

B. 1896

C. 1902

D. 1930s

24. During the reigns of Elizabeth I and James I, the English government encouraged Scottish and English Protestants to settle in which Irish province?

A. Pale

B. Ulster

C. Grimsby

D. Dublin

ANSWERS TO TESTS

Answers to tests

ANSWERS TO TEST 1:

1. A – 2.C – 3.B – 4.C – 5.B – 6.D – 7.C,D – 8.D – 9.B – 10.A – 11.B,C – 12.B – 13.B – 14.A – 15.B – 16.C – 17.C – 18.A – 19.A – 20.B – 21.A – 22.D – 23.A – 24.C

ANSWERS TO TEST 2:

1.A – 2.A,D – 3.C – 4.A – 5.A,B – 6.A – 7.C – 8.A,C – 9.D. – 10.A – 11.B – 12.B – 13.A,B – 14.B – 15.C – 16.C – 17.A – 18.D – 19.C – 20.A – 21.A – 22.A – 23.B – 24.A

ANSWERS TO TEST 3:

1.D – 2.A – 3.A – 4.A – 5.C – 6.B – 7.A,D – 8.B – 9.B – 10.A – 11.B – 12.A – 13.C – 14.A,B – 15.B – 16.A – 17.B – 18.B – 19.B – 20.C – 21.B – 22.D – 23.B – 24.A,B

ANSWERS TO TEST 4:

1.B – 2.B,D – 3.D – 4.C – 5.D – 6.A – 7.A – 8.A – 9.A – 10.D – 11.C – 12.D – 13.B – 14.B – 15.B – 16.A,B – 17.D – 18.A – 19.A – 20.B – 21.A – 22.A – 23.D – 24.D

ANSWERS TO TEST 5:

1.A – 2.B – 3.B – 4.B – 5.B – 6.C – 7.B – 8.A – 9.B – 10.C – 11.B – 12.D – 13.A – 14.B – 15.B – 16.A,D – 17.A – 18.A,B – 19.A – 20.C – 21.B – 22.B – 23.A – 24.A

ANSWERS TO TEST 6:

1.B,C – 2.C – 3.B – 4.A,B – 5.A – 6.A – 7.A – 8.A – 9.A,B – 10.A,D – 11.B – 12.A – 13.B,D – 14.A,D – 15.C,D – 16.A – 17.C – 18.C – 19.B – 20.B – 21.A – 22.C – 23.A – 24.C

ANSWERS TO TEST 7:

1.B – 2.A – 3.B – 4.A,B – 5.D – 6.A,D – 7.A – 8.D – 9.B – 10.C – 11.A – 12.B – 13.B – 14.C,D – 15.A,D – 16.B – 17.B – 18.C – 19.A – 20.A – 21.B – 22.A,B – 23.C – 24.B

ANSWERS TO TEST 8:

1.C – 2.A – 3.D – 4.B – 5.A,B – 6.A – 7.D – 8.C – 9.B – 10.C – 11.B – 12.C – 13.D – 14.B – 15.C – 16.A – 17.C – 18.D – 19.B,C – 20.B – 21.A – 22.B – 23.A – 24.C

ANSWERS TO TEST 9:

1.B,C – 2.B – 3.B – 4.A – 5.B – 6.B – 7.C – 8.B – 9.B – 10.C – 11.D – 12.C – 13.A – 14.A – 15.B – 16.B – 17.A – 18.A – 19.C – 20.B – 21.B – 22.A – 23.D – 24.D

ANSWER TO TEST 10:

1.B – 2.C – 3.B – 4.C – 5.B – 6.A – 7.A – 8.A – 9.A – 10.B,C – 11.D – 12.C – 13.D – 14.A – 15.B – 16.C – 17.A – 18.B – 19.A – 20.B,C – 21.D – 22.A – 23.C – 24.D

ANSWER TO TEST 11:

1.C – 2.D – 3.D – 4.C – 5.D – 6.D – 7.A – 8.A – 9.B – 10.A – 11.A – 12.D – 13.A,C – 14.D – 15.D – 16.D – 17.A – 18.D – 19.B – 20.A – 21.D – 22.B – 23.A – 24.B

ANSWER TO TEST 12:

1.A – 2.A – 3.A,B – 4.A – 5.B – 6.A – 7.B,C – 8.B – 9.B,D – 10.C – 11.B – 12.D – 13.B – 14.C – 15.C – 16.C – 17.A – 18.A – 19.B,D – 20.A – 21.A – 22.C – 23.C – 24.B

This is it. You have worked hard and you are now ready to take the real test.

Now, it is time to celebrate all your hard work, have a drink, take a deep breath and pat yourself on the back. You will be walking to the testing centre with the confidence to pass.

Thank you for buying this guide and best of luck!

Please, do remember to leave a review and some feedback for this Book. Every little helps, I really appreciate that you decided to purchase this book. Your feedback will help improve future editions.

Thank you.

Hugh L.

Printed in Great Britain
by Amazon